THELEMIC SUTRAS

IAO131

☉ 0°♊, May 2013 e.v.,
Anno IV *xxi*, the 109th year of the New Aeon

THELEMA SUTRAS

BY IAO131

First Edition (2013, e.v.)
Anno IV *xxi*, the 109th Year of the New Aeon

Cover art by:
Mustafa Al-Laylah

Other art by:
IAO131

TABLE OF CONTENTS

Table of Contents . . . . *i*

Preface: The Face you had Before you were Born . . . . . *iv*

PART I: THELEMA UPANISHADS

Chapter 1: Introduction to Thelema Upanishads . . . 1

Chapter 2: Gnarled Oak Upanishad 5

Chapter 3: Drop of Divine Dew Upanishad 13

Chapter 4: Unmoved Mover Upanishad 15

Chapter 5: Supreme Self Upanishad 22

Chapter 6: Ten Disciples Upanishad 24

Chapter 7: Inner King Upanishad 44

Chapter 8: Secret of Death Upanishad 47

Chapter 9: Great Word Upanishad 72

AN INCREDIBLY LONG INTERLUDE:
THE LOST SUTRA OF HAROLD

Introduction 79

Part 1: The Bursting-Forth of Harold from the
Great Womb of Time 81

Part 2: From the Mouth of Babes Comes a lot
of Nonsense 84

Part 3: The Precepts and Percepts of a Lonely
Pedestrian upon the Path of Perfection 87

Part 4: The Inexorable Mutability of Phenomena,
or how Harold Achieved the Grade of $2°=9^\square$ . . . 90

Part 5: The Tavern of Spiritual Intoxication, and
how Harold Forsaked Buddhism 94

Part 6: The Ironies of Isis, or the Uncovering of
the Contradiction known as Man 97

Part 7: The Pistol of Pragmatism, or how Harold
Executed Two Traitors to their own Tenets . . . 102

Part 8: Superfice is Super-nice, and other Failed
Attempts at Cleverness 108

Part 9: A Prod is always better than *A Priori,* or
how Harold exposed the Nether-Regions
of Philosophy 113

Part 10: Not Two and Certainly not Three or
Four, or how Harold became an
Advaita Vedantist 118

Part 11: Harold Practices Spiritual Optomery as
a Wandering Prophet Preaching from the
Positionless Position 122

Part 12: Everything is Completely Arbitrary
but Nonetheless Beautiful, and other Watch-
words of Harold's Attainment 125

Part 13: The Re-Establishment of the Reality
of Hallucination, or how Harold became
a Butterfly 130

Part 14: Harold Weaves, and is Clothed with
Derision; Meditates, and is Plagued by Astral
Vision 136

Part 15: The Destructive Deity's Didactic
Delusions, or how Ra-Hoor-Khuit Tripped on
his Double-Wand of Power 140

Part 16: Terma Tupperware, or how Intuition
Guided Harold Astray 144
Part 17: Gluttony and Pride, or the Failings of
Magicians and Mystics 147
Part 18: Dissolve and Coagulate, or how Harold
Avoided Paying his Karmic Debt 149

PART II: THELEMA MADHYAMA-PRATIPAD
Chapter 1: Introduction to Thelema Madhyama-
Pratipad 154
Chapter 2: The Shadow Sermon 156
Chapter 3: The Diamond Teaching 160
Chapter 4: The Perfection of Understanding
Sutra 177
Chapter 5: A Commentary on The Perfection
of Understanding Sutra 180

Endnotes 236

Preface:
The face you had before you were born

Do what thou wilt shall be the whole of the Law.

Thelema Sutras? What kind of nonsense is this? Well, in short, it's the kind of nonsense I enjoy writing.

Sutras are Eastern texts, specifically those of Hinduism and Buddhism. They come in many forms and many styles, but they represent the various manifestations of the Light of the Gnosis as they appeared throughout the East. I personally view Thelema as more than simply being in the Western Mystery Tradition or being the next Divine Covenant after Islam. Much of Thelema involves uniting and transcending opposites, and the East-West dichotomy is one of these. It therefore occurred to me to approach the self-same Mysteries but with the style and attitude of someone from the East rather than the typical Western Hermetic-Qabalistic-Occultist approach.

Sutras are defined in the Vedas as being "Of minimal syllabary, unambiguous, pithy, comprehensive, continuous, and without flaw: who knows the sutra knows it to be thus." While it is debatable whether or not any sutras actually accomplish this lofty ideal, their intent and approach are nonetheless made clear with this definition. Before we begin on our unambiguous flawlessness with minimal syllabary, I'd like to say a little bit about myself and my approach:

One common misunderstanding I have encountered about my writing is that people think I believe everything I write is true. At this point in time, I can't even count the amount of times that someone has said, "I've read some of your writings, and I don't agree with everything in there," to which my inevitable response is, "Yeah, I don't agree with everything in there either." I am constantly learning and growing, I am still a student among students, and if I believed I already knew everything, I would be stagnant and, worst of all, terrifyingly bored.

I write about various topics and I use various styles. To me, writing is more than just a medium for conveying information. Writing is an art-form. Just like other art, it has rhythm and texture, it has different styles and genres, and it evokes a subjective response in those who experience it. The art of writing is to evoke new feelings, perspectives, and ideas in the reader; it isn't to convey Truth... as if that were even possible. I don't even believe in The Truth – I believe in *my* Truth, which can never be quite the same as *your* Truth. One of the beauties of the Law of Thelema is the acknowledgment of each individual having their own Truth.

The various sutras of Hinduism and Buddhism had a large impact on me very early on my Path to accomplish the Great Work. Although I did not believe every metaphysical and ethical proposition that was espoused, I have found they create a certain state of mind in me by a sort of resonance. The high-flung but succinct language of the Upanishads, the inspiring and self-assured language of the Bhagavad Gita, the clarity and repetitiousness of the Dhammapada, the strange and paradoxical sutras of Zen... all of these texts have a slightly different effect, but they all work the Magick of causing a change in consciousness that is resonant with the topic at hand.

When reading the Upanishads, I may feel like a jnana yogi, piercing through the ignorance of the dualistic mind with expansive clarity; when reading the Bhagavad Gita, I may feel inspired and encouraged to fight the spiritual battle against my lower nature and conquer the Universe through meditation; when reading the Dhammapada, I may feel calmed and moved to live a balanced and controlled life; when reading the Zen sutras, I may feel like a conqueror of the lopsided insistence of the rational mind and often get a bit of a headache while I'm at it.

For this to work, one has to almost pre-assume the truth of what one is reading. This is not to discard one's rationality but, rather, to put it aside for a moment so that the usual constant critiques – the "that's not what I've read"s and the "that isn't necessarily so"s – are put on pause <u>to appreciate the text as it is and its effect on oneself</u>. It is absurd to say a musical piece or sculpture or painting is "not true" in any kind of realistic sense beyond "it does not resonate with me." In this case, it is not part of *your* Truth... but it would be insane for you or anyone else to insist that no one can or should enjoy a song because you do not. Yet this is exactly what is done by most people when reading anything that isn't a novel.

All I can humbly ask of you, dear reader, is that you put away your preconceptions, your knowledge about Thelema, your undoubtedly extensive knowledge of the Qabalistic Tree of Life, and everything else that leaves your cup pre-filled... and just have a child-mind while reading this material.

Writing is my art-form, and my subject matter is Thelema. Therefore, every piece I write – whether it is a scholarly essay, magical ceremony, dithyrambic diatribe, poetic explosion, or whatever else – is simply one lens through which we may look at Thelema. The intent is not to create an internally consistent structure of logical arguments; it is not even to construct a system of any kind. Like Nietzsche, I mistrust all systematizers, and, like Blake, I feel that I must create my own system or be enslaved by another's... and it must be created anew time and time again or else I will be enslaved by my own structure.

For me, wanting an unchanging and infallible structure is a sign of anxiety and of weakness. The world is ambiguous; She is in perpetual and constant flux, and any attempt to constrain Her for the satisfaction of our petty mind's insistence on order and understandability seems genuinely unfair to Her. I was going to say "childish," but – if anything – it is more "oldish": to insist on absolute structure is calcified, stagnant, scared, tired.

It is the Aeon of the Child and, like children, I believe we should engage in play – play with different words, different ideas, and different perspectives. This book is nothing other than play, and I am simply inviting you to come along with me. If you see something a different way, have a new train of thought, are lifted into a meditative head-space, or even just have a little fun, then my work will have accomplished its intended purpose even though I am (of course!) "delivered from the lust of result."

In the name of the Ineffable None,

Frater IAO131

Love is the law, love under will.

Part I:
Thelema Upanishads

CHAPTER 1:
INTRODUCTION TO
THELEMA UPANISHADS

The Hindu Upanishads represent a storehouse of the esoteric doctrine of the Self (*Atman*) being one with the un-differentiated, boundless Reality (*Brahman*) of Being, Consciousness, and Bliss (*sat-chit-ananda*). This idea is sometimes stated as "Atman is Brahman" or "Thou art That." This wisdom is timeless although the names and forms thereof are continually uprooted, interchanged, and transformed. These Thelema Upanishads are based on the Hindu versions in spirit, and they have been adapted and revised to be resonant with the Law of this New Aeon of the Crowned & Conquering Child, Horus.

Though this wisdom comes from Hinduism, it is, in various ways, no different from the wisdom that comes from Buddhism, from Judeo-Christian-Islamic mystics, or from Thelema itself. All roads may lead to Rome, so to speak, but the nature of the different paths, including the sights seen along the way, are all different. Each path has a different language, a different set of symbols, and a different emphasis. Behind all these various veils is a single Light. As it has been said, "Now the Great Work is one, and the Initiation is one, and the Reward is one, <u>however diverse are the symbols</u> <u>wherein the Unutterable is clothed.</u>"[1] Also, in our Holy Books: "To you who yet wander in the Court of the Profane we cannot yet reveal all; but you will easily understand that the religions of the world are but symbols and veils of the Absolute Truth. So also are the philosophies. To the adept, seeing all these things from above, there seems nothing to choose between Buddha and Mohammed, between Atheism and Theism."[2]

Thus, for example, while Buddha was famous for his notion of *anatta,* or "not-self," I see no particular contradiction with the Hindu focus on *atman,* or "self." Though, on the face of it, they appear as exact opposites, they get at the same message, the same Truth. Buddhism proceeds negatively, by denying this Truth any categories or labels of which we can conceive, and Hinduism proceeds positively, by asserting this Truth by any and all categories or labels. This, too, is not exactly true. The various titles given to the *Atman* by Hindu sages are virtually identical to those given by Mahayana Buddhists to the *Dharmakaya,* or "truth body," as well as *Buddhadhatu,* or "Buddha-nature." Conversely, Hindu sages – particularly those of Advaita Vedanta and *jnana* Yoga – are famous for saying "*neti, neti,*" or "not this, not that." By this, they deny the

[2]

Atman as having any qualities in the same fashion that Buddhists deny any qualities given to *shunyata,* "emptiness."

I know that theologians and philosophers will have many quarrels with what I have written above. Some have drawn distinctions between the *moksha,* or "liberation," of Hindus and the *nirvana* of Buddhists, between *samadhi* and *nirodha-sampatti,* et cetera ad infinitum. I have basically used Horus as a symbol of *Atman* throughout these texts, but people will inevitably say "No, that is the Holy Guardian Angel," or "No, that is Hadit." If we take the Holy Guardian Angel as Tiphareth, Horus as Kether, and Hadit as the 0 beyond even Kether, we see that they are all reflections of one another. The insistence on classifying and categorizing everything makes me feel a bit dirty; I know that it is trying to fit a round peg into a Tree of Life-shaped hole. Personally, I find little to no use of these intellectual classifications and philosophical arguments. Whatever the intellect may think or classify or debate, the goal of both Buddhism and Hinduism is beyond the intellect. *Solvitur ambulando* – "it is solved by walking" – and it is instructive that most theologians and philosophers find it hard to do their jobs while walking. Even the best map-maker may have no working knowledge of avoiding the dangers and finding the best pathways on the actual path. AKA one should do & be

Let us view these various texts, then, as prods goading us to action, as fingers pointing to the moon. Woe unto them who merely study the prod and the finger! Woe unto them who merely play with the Qabalistic correlations of action and the moon! Woe unto them who merely view this as a book to read and then to put down, mere "food for thought"! May they be brought from profane woe unto the sacred Whoa. Amen.

CHAPTER 2:
GNARLED OAK UPANISHAD[3]

"Gnarled Oak of God!

In thy branches is the lightning nested!

Above thee hangs the Eyeless Hawk."

–Liber A'ash vel Capricorni Pneumatici

PART 1

A wife loves her husband not just for his own sake, but because the True Self of Horus plays through him.[4]

A husband loves his wife not just for her own sake, but because the True Self plays through her.

Children are loved not just for their own sake, but because the True Self plays through them.

Wealth is loved not just for its own sake, but because the True Self plays through it.

Philosophers, adepts, and masters are loved not just for their own sake, but because the True Self plays through them.

Warriors are loved not just for their own sake, but because the True Self plays through them.

The universe is loved not just for its own sake, but because the True Self plays through it.

The astral beings are loved not just for their own sake, but because the True Self plays through them.

The earthly creatures are loved not just for their own sake, but because the True Self plays through them.

Everything is loved just not for its own sake, but because the True Self plays through it.

This Self, the Crowned and Conquering Child, has to be realized. Hear about this Self and meditate upon It, Child of Earth. When you hear about the Self, meditate upon the Self, and – finally realizing the Self – you come to understand everything in life as Limitless Light and Pure Joy, True Wisdom and Perfect Happiness.[5]

For philosophers', adepts', and masters' words confuse, making one regard them as separate from this Self. Warriors' actions confuse, making one regard them as separate from this Self. Astral beings' and earthly creatures' appearances confuse, making one regard them as separate from this Self. The universe's appearance confuses, making one regard it as separate from this Self. Everything confuses those who regard things as separate from this Self.

Philosophers, adepts, masters, warriors, astral beings, earthly creatures, the universe, everything: these are the Self.

As a lump of salt thrown in water dissolves and cannot be taken out again, even so the separate self or 'ego' dissolves in the identity with Horus: a sea of pure consciousness, infinite, and immortal.

As blood drained out into the Universal Life in the Cup of Babalon[6] dissolves and cannot be taken out again, even so the separate self or 'ego' dissolves in the identity with Horus: a pulse of pure consciousness, infinite, and immortal.

The notion of separateness – one's self being separate from the True Self of Horus – arises from identifying oneself with the body, which is made up of the temporary physical elements; when this physical identification dissolves, there can be no more separate self.] *yoga is forgetting the body*

The notion of separateness – one's self being separate from the True Self of Horus – arises from identifying oneself with thoughts, which are made up of the temporary mental elements;

[7]

when this mental identification dissolves, there can be no more separate self.[7]

Are you bewildered when I say there is no separate self? [As long as there is separateness, one sees, hears, smells, feels, speaks to, thinks of, and knows another as separate from oneself.] But when the Self is realized as the indivisible Unity of Life, the continuity of existence, who can be seen by whom?[8] Has it not been said to bind nothing and let there be no difference made among you between any one thing and any other thing?[9] Who can be heard by whom? [Who can be smelled by, felt by, spoken to, thought of, or known by whom?] In this state, how can the knower ever be known? It is not known if it be known.[10]

AUMGN. AUMGN. AUMGN.

PART 2

Several questions were once put forward to a Master of the Temple, for there were many sages with great knowledge but she had Understanding.

The first question was, "What are all things in the world - past, present, and future - woven in?"

[8]

The answer came as "Space," which satisfied the questioner.

Then the second question came, "In what is Space woven?"

The answer came:

> "Those who are Knowing call it the Crowned and Conquering Child, the Imperishable.[11]
>
> It is neither big nor small, long nor short, hot nor cold, moist nor dry, bright nor dark, neither air nor space.[12] It is without attachment, sound, taste, smell, sight, or touch, without mouth, ears, tongue, nose, eyes, body, breath, or mind. It is without movement, limitation, inside, or outside. It consumes nothing, and nothing consumes It.
>
> In perfect accord with the Will of Horus the Deathless,[13] the sun and moon make their orbits; the zodiac turns in the skies; heaven and earth remain in place; moments, hours, days, nights, weeks, months, and seasons become years; plants are born, live, die, and reborn.
>
> This Imperishable Hawk of Light is the seer, though It is unseen; the hearer, though unheard, the thinker, though unthought, the knower, though unknown. Nothing other than the Imperishable can see, hear think, or know. It is in this

Crowned and Conquering Child, the Imperishable Substance, wherein Space is woven."

This same Master, earthly emissary of the Crowned and Conquering Child-King, was questioned again by another authority. He spoke:

> "The Sun is the light of mankind by which we rise, go out, work, and come back. When the sun sets, the moon is the light of mankind. When the moon sets, fire is the light of mankind. When fire goes out, speech is the light of mankind. When the sun and moon set, the fire goes out, and no one speaks, what is the light of mankind?"

The Master of the Temple replied:

> "The Self, the Hawk-Headed Lord of Silence and Strength, is the True Light of mankind, by which we rise, go out, work, and eventually return.
>
> Horus is pure, undifferentiated awareness,[14] and He shines as the light within the heart, surrounded by the senses. Only seeming to think, seeming to move, the Supreme Self neither sleeps nor wakes nor dreams. Abiding in this Self, one is free from desire, free from good and evil, free from hope and from fear.[15]

As a man in the arms of his beloved is not aware of what is without and what is within, so a person in union with his own True Self is not aware of what is without and what is within, for in that Unitive State all desires find their perfect fulfillment.[16] There is no other desire that needs to be fulfilled, and one goes beyond sorrow.[17]

In that Unitive State there is neither father nor mother, neither worlds nor people nor even the scriptures of Law. In that state there is neither slayer nor slain, neither low nor high, neither sacred nor profane.

This Self is beyond good and evil, beyond all the suffering of the human condition. In that Unitive State, one sees without seeing and knows without knowing, for one is alone and there is nothing separate from Oneself.[18]

Where there is separateness and multiplicity, one sees, smells, tastes, speaks to, hears, touches, thinks of, and knows another. But where there is Unity, One without a Two, that is the world of Horus, Lord of Limitless Light and Love![19] This is the supreme goal of life, the supreme treasure, the supreme Joy; it is the Summum Bonum, the Great Work.[20] Those who do not seek this supreme goal live on but a fraction of this Joy. They feel little, and what is, is balanced by weak joys.[21]

[The Self is indeed Horus, but through ignorance people identify themselves with intellect, mind, senses, passions, and the physical elements.]This is why Horus, the True Self, is said to consist of this and that, and appears to be everything.[22]

When all the fool's knots that strangle the heart are loosened, the mortal becomes immortal – even now and here in this very life.[23] As the skin of a snake is discarded, so does the normal self die; but the True Self, freed from identification with the body and the mind, merges in Horus: infinite Light, eternal Life, inexhaustible Love, boundless Liberty.

Those who realize this Self enter into the Peace that brings complete self-control and perfect patience.[24] They see Themselves in everyone and everyone in Themselves.[25] Evil cannot overcome them because They overcome all evil. Sin cannot consume them because They consume all sin. Death cannot destroy them because They destroy death.

Free from the evil of duality, free from sin of separateness, free from the delusion of the death-condemned ego, They live in the Kingdom of the Crowned and Conquering Child. Children of Earth, this Kingdom is Yours! Rejoice!

AUMGN. AUMGN. AUMGN.

CHAPTER 3:
DROP OF DIVINE DEW
UPANISHAD[26]

"How the dew of the Universe whitens the lips!"

–Liber Liberi vel Lapidus Lazuli

Let us meditate on the shining True Self: changeless, underlying the world of change, and realized in the heart in Knowledge and Conversation.[27]

This supreme Goal is hard to reach, hard to describe, and hard to abide in. [They alone attain Knowledge and Conversation who have mastered their senses, and are free from emotional fluctuations, free from likes and dislikes, without selfish bonds to people, things, and self-identity.[28]]

They alone attain Knowledge and Conversation who are prepared to face challenge after challenge in Magick and Meditation. With undaunted persistence and one-pointed concentration, they become united with Horus, the Lord of Love.[29] Called Ra-Hoor-Khuit, who is present everywhere, the three dimensions of space emanate from Him, although He is infinite and invisible. Though all the galaxies and stars emerge from Him, He is without form and unconditioned.

To be united with Horus, the Lord of Love, is to be freed from all restriction. This is the state of Self-realization, far beyond the reach of words and thoughts. To be united with Horus, one's Angel and Inmost Self – imperishable, changeless, beyond cause and effect – is to find infinite Joy.[30] Ra-Hoor-Khuit is beyond all duality, beyond the reach of 'thinker' and 'thought.'

Let us meditate on our True Shining Self, the ultimate reality, who is realized by Adepts in Knowledge and Conversation.

One's True Self cannot be realized by those who are subject to fear, regret, pity, and sorrow. The Lord of Silence cannot be realized by those who are subject to pride of name and fame or to the vanity of scholarship. It cannot be realized by those who cling to titles, both secular and occult. It cannot be realized by those who are enmeshed in life's duality.

But to all those who pierce this duality,[31] whose hearts are given to the Lord of Love: He gives Himself through His infinite wrath; He gives Himself through His infinite grace.

AUMGN. AUMGN. AUMGN.

CHAPTER 4:
UNMOVED MOVER UPANISHAD32

"I am the Magician and the Exorcist.

I am the axle of the wheel, and the cube in the circle.

'Come unto me' is a foolish word: for it is I that go."

–Liber AL vel Legis

The student asks:

"Who makes my mind think?

Who fills my body with energy to act?

Who causes my tongue to speak?

Who is that invisible one who sees through my eyes?

Who is it that hears through my ears?"

The teacher responds:

"Horus is the Supreme Self.

This Self is the ear of the ear, the eye of the eye, the nose of the nose, the tongue of the tongue, the word of words, the mind of mind, and the life of life.

Transcending the five senses and the thoughts of the mind, renouncing the separate existence of the ego, the wise realize the Deathless Self.

Our eyes cannot see this Self, our words cannot express this Self; this Self cannot even be grasped by the thoughts of the mind. We do not know, we cannot know, because this Self is different from the known and different from the unknown. Thus say all illumined and wise ones.

That which moves the tongue to speak but cannot be found in any words spoken by the tongue: know *that* as the Self. This Self is not someone other than you. Thou art That.

That which moves the eye to see but cannot be found in any sights of the eye, that is the Self. This Self is not someone other than you. Thou art That.

That which moves the mind to think but cannot be found in any thoughts of the mind, that is the Self. This Self is not someone other than you. Thou art That.

That which moves the body to draw breath but cannot be found in the body or in the breath, that is the Self. This Self is not someone other than you. Thou art That.

If you think, "I know the Self," you do not know the Self. It is beyond the knower and the known. Therefore, It is not known if it be known.[33] All you can see is His external form. Therefore, continue your meditation!"

The student replies:

"I do not think I know the Self, nor can I truly say that I do not know him."

The teacher responds:

"There is only one way to truly know the Self, and that is to realize the Self yourself.

The ignorant and profane think the Self can be known by the intellect. The wise and illuminated know that he is beyond the duality of knower and known.

[The Self is realized in a transcendent state of consciousness, only once you have broken through the identification with the senses of the body and the thoughts of the mind.]The senses and thoughts are subject to birth and death. To realize and be the Self is go beyond death. One thereby destroys the destroyer.[34]

Realize this Supreme Self in meditation, the radiant and effulgent goal of all life! The supreme attainment of Love! If you do not realize this Self, there is only darkness. See the Self in all things, become one with this Self! Then all the gods even and death will tremble before You![35]

Let me tell you a story:

Once upon a time, the Three Powers – Typhon, Hermanubis, and the Sphinx[36] – defeated the demons of darkness in battle. Though this victory came only through the power of the Supreme Self, the Three Powers boasted, "The victory and splendor is ours! Ours is the power and the glory!"

The Self saw their pride and appeared before them unrecognized. They wondered who this being was, so Typhon – the god of Motion – approached him.

The mysterious being asked, "Who are you?"

"I am Typhon, god of Motion and Change, known to all."

"Are you powerful?"

"I can move all on earth."

"Move this." The Self placed a single mote of dust on the ground. Typhon struck and attacked the mote of dust, using all his force, but he failed to move it. He ran back to the other two Powers and confessed, "I have failed to discover the identity of this strange being." Hermanubis – the god of Stillness – then approached the Self.

The mysterious being asked, "Who are you?"

"I am Hermanubis, god of Stillness and Rest, known to all."

"Are you powerful?"

"I can bring all things on earth to a halt."

"Stop this." The Self then picked up the mote of dust and it swayed to and fro in the air. Hermanubis threw all of his powers upon the mote of dust but could not cause it to become still. He ran back to the other two Powers and confessed, "I have failed to discover the identity of this strange being." The Sphinx – the god of Balance – then approached the Self.

Upon being approached, the mysterious being disappeared and a Hermit, a sage of great wisdom, appeared in the being's place. The Sphinx asked the Hermit, "Who was that being?"

The Hermit replied, "That was Horus, from whom comes all your splendor and victory, all your power and glory. [You

Three Powers turn the Wheel of Life but all depends from the axle of this wheel, the point in the center, who is Horus, the Lord of Limitless Love, of Limitless Light." The Three Powers realized at last that their true Self is Horus, the Supreme Self."

The student insisted:

"Teach me more of your spiritual wisdom."

The teacher continued:

"The light of Horus flashes in lightning, and the light of Horus flashes in our eyes. As above, so below.[37]

It is the power of the Supreme and Boundless Self that makes the mind to think, to seek, to desire, and to will. Therefore, use this very power to meditate on the Self.

Horus is the inmost Self of everyone, he burns in the heart of everyone and at the core of every star.[38] This Self alone is worthy of all our Love; It is the sole goal of all Magick. Meditate upon this Self in all. Those who meditate upon the Self are loved by all.

Discipline of the mind in fixed thought, non-attachment to the five senses and material events, strength and control of the animal passions, discipline of the emotions and the intellect, and the Love of all are the body of a true Magician.[39] The Holy Books are the limbs of a true Magician. The Truth is the very heart of this true Magician.

Those who realize Horus shall conquer all, both good and evil, and attain the Supreme State of Unity. Truly, they shall conquer all and attain the Supreme State!

AUMGN. AUMGN. AUMGN.

CHAPTER 5:
SUPREME SELF UPANISHAD[40]

"In the name of the Lord of Initiation, Amen."

–Liber Tzaddi vel Hamus Hermeticus

Ra-Hoor-Khuit manifests in three ways: the outer, the inner, and the Supreme Self.

Flesh, spine, hair, fingers, toes, nails, feet, ankles, shins, knees, thighs, groin, hips, navel, stomach, chest, shoulders, arms, hands, fingers, neck, chin, mouth, nose, forehead, eyes, ears, hair, blood vessels, nerves: these make up the outer self, the body, subject to birth and to death.

The inner self perceives the outside world, made up of the various elements. The inner self is the victim of likes and dislikes, pleasure and pain, ignorance, sorrow, regret, pity, fear, and doubt. It knows all the subtleties of language and knowledge, enjoys food, drink, dance, music, and all the fine arts, delights in the senses, recalls the past, looks to the future, reads the scriptures, and is able to act. This is the mind, the inner person, subject to birth and to death.

The Supreme Self, adored in the Holy Books, can be realized through the path of Union in Magick and Yoga. Subtler than the smallest seed, subtler than the smallest mote of dust, subtler than the hundred-thousandth part of a hair, subtler even than an atom: [this Supreme Self cannot be mentally grasped; it cannot be physically seen.]

The Supreme Self is neither born nor dies. It cannot be burned, wet, moved, pierced, cut nor dried. Beyond all attributes, the Supreme Self is the eternal witness, ever pure, indivisible, deathless, and uncompounded, far beyond the senses and the ego. In this Self, conflicts and expectations cease. It is omnipresent, beyond all thought, beyond all time, beyond all space, without action in the external world, without action in the internal world. [Beyond the outer and the inner, this Supreme Self purifies the impure.]

AUMGN. AUMGN. AUMGN.

CHAPTER 6:
TEN DISCIPLINES UPANISHAD[41]

"Thy one crown of all the Ten

Even now and here be mine.

AMEN."

–The Book of Lies

The disciple asked:

"You speak with great wisdom about the Supreme Self, but how may we attain to this illumination?"

The sage answered:

"The foundation for this illumination is laid through the cultivation of the Ten Disciplines. These Ten Disciplines are like the two hands of a true Master, each with five offshoots, like fingers on your hands. The two hands of Discipline are Control and Virtue.[42] The five fingers of Control are non-violence, non-falsity, non-stealing, non-hoarding, and non-lusting.[43] The five fingers of Virtue are cleanliness, contentment, spiritual practice, study of the Holy Books, and self-surrender."[44]

The disciple pleaded:

"Please speak further of the five fingers of Control."

The sage replied:

"One half of Control is to recognize a delusion as a delusion. The other half of Control is to not think, speak, or act out of that delusion. Together, recognition and restraint are the entirety of Control. The five fingers on the hand of Control are non-violence, non-falsity, non-stealing, non-hoarding, and non-lusting. These five fingers are merely important cases to help you understand Control through elaboration."

The disciple said:

"I understand, wise one. Please speak further of the first finger of Control, non-violence."

The sage explained:

"The first finger on the hand of Control is non-violence. Abstain from causing pain, harm, and suffering to others. This means abstain from causing harm in thought, word, and deed."

The disciple interjected:

"But, wise one, we may never know what deeds may harm others. Even with a deep inhalation, we may kill many insects. Even with a well-intentioned word, we may cause suffering in another."

The sage answered:

"This is certainly true, disciple, certainly unavoidable. Yet non-violence does not mean avoid all possibility of harm at all costs, for then one would need to lock oneself in a cage and never speak a word. And even this non-action and silence may cause suffering!

To practice the Control of non-violence is not to worry whether anything has caused harm – this is mere reaction. To practice the Control of non-violence is to see that no thought, word, or deed is birthed within you whose intent or purpose is to cause harm.

The root of violence is anger, which is fed by the waters of ego. Were you to realize the Supreme Self that abides in all, you would see no ultimate difference between yourself and others, and no anger would therefore ever arise. To practice violence is to feed the delusion of separateness. To practice non-violence is to cultivate the wisdom of non-separateness.

Therefore, to practice non-violence, be mindful of all anger within you. If this anger gives birth to an act of violence, promptly apologize to him to whom you have done violence, and practice ten acts of kindness for every act of violence. If this anger gives birth to a word of violence, promptly apologize to him to whom you have spoken violence, and speak ten words of kindness for every word of violence. If this anger gives birth to a thought of violence, apologize to him to whom you have thought violence, and think ten thoughts of kindness for every thought of violence.

Since the Supreme Self abides in all, when you practice violence, you are truly doing violence to yourself, and when you practice kindness, this is kindness to yourself. Thus is the Control of non-violence cultivated, disciple."

The disciple said:

"Thank you, wise sage. Please speak further on the second finger of Control, non-falsity."

The sage replied:

"The second finger on the hand of Control is non-falsity. Abstain from all falsity in thought, word, and deed."

The disciple interjected:

"But, wise one, we may never know what deeds may be false. Even a well-intentioned act may prove to be the wrong course. Even a word spoken earnestly may prove to be false."

The sage answered:

"This is certainly true, disciple, certainly unavoidable. Yet non-falsity does not mean avoid all possibility of falsity at all costs, for then one would need to lock oneself in a cage and never speak a word. And even this non-action and silence may prove false!

To practice the Control of non-falsity is not to worry whether anything will prove false – this is mere reaction. To practice the Control of non-falsity is to see that no thought, word, or deed is birthed within you whose intent or purpose is to be false.

The root of falsity is cleverness, which is fed by the waters of ego. Only in thinking we can get the better of someone would we think, speak, or act out of falsity. Were you to realize the Supreme Self that abides in all, you would see no ultimate difference between yourself and others, and no cleverness would therefore ever arise. To practice falsity is to feed the delusion of separateness. To practice non-falsity is to cultivate the wisdom of non-separateness.]

Therefore, to practice non-falsity, be mindful of all cleverness within you. If this cleverness gives birth to an act of falsity, promptly apologize to him to whom you have done falsity, and practice ten acts of truth for every act of falsity. If this cleverness gives birth to a word of falsity, promptly apologize to him to whom you have spoken falsity, and speak ten words of truth for every word of falsity. If this cleverness gives birth to a thought of falsity, apologize to him to whom you have thought falsity, and think ten thoughts of truth for every thought of falsity.

Since the Supreme Self abides in all, when you practice falsity, you are truly being false to yourself, and when you practice truth, this is truth to yourself. Thus is how the Control of non-falsity cultivated, disciple.]

The same is basically true for the next two fingers of Control, non-stealing and non-hoarding. Non-stealing means to not steal from others, not even to think about stealing. To steal is to admit that you want something you do not have, it is to assert a duality. To hoard means to not cling to what you do have. To hoard is to admit that you want to never let go of what you do have. To steal is to be attached to what you do not have. To hoard is to be attached to what you do have. If you find that you even so much as think of stealing or think of hoarding, you should then give ten things away to others for every thought of stealing and hoarding.

Neither of these things are evil, disciple, neither stealing nor hoarding, as the Supreme Self abides in all. Nonetheless, they are not conducive to your practice. This Supreme Self is beyond all attachment, and if you practice attachment every day, you will not realize this Self. Even so, if you are starving, it is better to steal bread and return to meditation than to constantly think about your hunger during meditation. If you are freezing in the cold, it is better to cling to your last coat to remain warm for your meditation than to give it up and constantly think about your coldness during meditation. Be resolute, disciple, but never inflexible; stay true to the principles of Control without sabotaging yourself."

The disciple said:

"Thank you, wise sage. Please speak further of the fifth finger of Control, non-lusting."

The sage explained:

"Non-lusting is the final finger on the hand of Control. When a man is consumed by lust, he can not think about anything other than that for which he lusts. His lower nature drives his thoughts, words, and deeds. [How much more satisfied he would be if this energy were turned to the object of his meditation rather than the object of his lusts!]

Lust should not be killed, it cannot be killed, but it can be controlled. At your stage, disciple, it is best to learn to control lust. The Control of non-lusting means be aware whenever even the smallest thought is birthed within you from lust. Lust, like all delusions, will arise and then it will disappear. You must recognize the lust and then neither act nor speak, not even think, out of this lust. This is the Control of non-lusting.

Non-violence, non-falsity, non-stealing, non-hoarding, and non-lusting are the five fingers of Control that will aid in laying the foundation for the realization of your Supreme Self. Restrain yourself from all violence, all falsity, all stealing, all hoarding, and all lusting. Practice Control in thought, in word, and in deed. This is the hand of Control.

Nonetheless, remember that the five fingers of Control are mere knowledge, not truth. The only Truth is the Supreme

Self. Realize It! Knowledge is like a raft that leads to the shore of Truth. You do not need a raft once you have reached your destination, yet you cannot reach your destination without a raft. This raft is built of the knowledge of Control, it is guided by the knowledge of Virtue, and the destination is the Truth of the Supreme Self. Realize It!"

The disciple said:

"I bow in obeisance to you, great sage. Please speak further on the five fingers of Virtue."

The sage replied:

"One half of Virtue is to recognize virtue as virtue. The other half of Virtue is to express all thought, speech, and action out of that virtue. Together, recognition and expression are the entirety of Virtue. [The five fingers on the hand of Virtue are cleanliness, contentment, spiritual practice, study of the Holy Books, and self-surrender.] These five fingers are merely important cases to help you understand Virtue through elaboration."

The disciple said:

"I understand, wise one. Please speak further of the first finger of Virtue, cleanliness."

The sage explained:

"The first finger on the hand of Virtue is cleanliness. This means cleanliness of body, mind, and spirit. Primarily, cleanliness of the body is to practice the five fingers of Control in all acts. Cleanliness of the body is, secondarily, to keep it healthy and strong, neither underfeeding or overfeeding it, neither being overly active nor overly docile.

Primarily, cleanliness of the mind is to practice the five fingers of Control in all speech. Cleanliness of the mind is, secondarily, to remember the goal of your meditation even in the midst of the many distracting elements of the world, especially the profane actions and profane speech of others.

Primarily, cleanliness of the spirit is to practice the five fingers of Control in all thought. Cleanliness of the spirit is to always be on guard against any distracting thoughts that may tempt you to swerve from the one object of your meditation, even in the midst of others."

The disciple asked:

"Wise sage, are there any marks of one who practices the Virtue of cleanliness?"

The sage replied:

"There is indeed a mark of one who practices the Virtue of cleanliness. Anyone who practices this Virtue will be buoyant and joyful; this is true religion. Anyone who does not practice this Virtue will be heavy and gloomy; this may be an upset stomach, but it is surely not true religion.

One who practices the Virtue of cleanliness will face the worst of adversities yet the defilement of sorrow will never crease a single wrinkle on their face. That is the mark of one who practices the Virtue of cleanliness."

The disciple pleaded:

"Please speak further on the second finger on the hand of Virtue, contentment."

The sage said:

"The second finger on the hand of Virtue is contentment. [Contentment means being satisfied with whatever one has had, whatever one has, and whatever one will have. This means non-attachment to all things that were, are, and are to come.]

With the Virtue of contentment, whatever happens that is bad is accepted without running away, and whatever happens that is good is accepted without running toward. Anger arises only when wishing to change what is; sloth arises only when wishing to refrain from changing what is. Lust arises only when wishing to have what one does not have; greed arises only when wishing to retain what one does have. Contentment is accepting what one does have without attachment, accepting what one does not have without attachment, and accepting whatever one may or may not have without attachment. This is how the Virtue of contentment is cultivated, disciple."

The disciple asked:

"Wise sage, are there any marks of one who practices the Virtue of contentment?"

The sage replied:

"There is indeed a mark of one who practices the Virtue of contentment. Anyone who practices this Virtue will be peaceful and patient. Anyone who does not practice this Virtue will be discontent and impatient. A placid face and a motionless foot are signs of one who practices this Virtue. A furrowed brow and a tapping foot are signs of one who fails to practice this Virtue.

One who practices the Virtue of contentment receives all blame without a single hair stirring on his head. One who practices the Virtue of contentment receives all praise without a single hair stirring on his head. One who practices this Virtue can receive all the riches of the world and not a single hair will stir on his head. One who practices this Virtue can lose all that he has in the world and not a single hair will stir on his head. Peace and patience in the face of adversity and of triumph is the mark of one who practices the Virtue of contentment. "

The disciple said:

"Please speak further on the third finger on the hand of Virtue, spiritual practice."

The sage replied:

"The third finger on the hand of Virtue is spiritual practice. Spiritual practice is essentially to sit and meditate. It is that simple. One who practices this Virtue actually performs his practices. One who does not practice this Virtue never actually performs his practices. To think about spiritual practice is not spiritual practice. To discuss, explain, or debate about spiritual practice is not spiritual practice. To practice is spiritual practice."

The disciple asked:

"Wise sage, are there any marks of one who practices the Virtue of spiritual practice?"

The sage replied:

"There is indeed a mark of one who practices the Virtue of spiritual practice. Anyone who practices this Virtue will be self-disciplined, which gives rise to silence and self-assuredness.

Whosoever practices this Virtue can explain all the intricacies of spiritual practice because it is derived from their extensive and persistent experience, but they do not speak about it because they would rather perform their spiritual practice. Whosoever does not practice this Virtue cannot explain all the intricacies of spiritual practice because they have no experience, but they constantly speak about it because of what they have read in books, because they seek to convince others of their spirituality, because speaking about spiritual practice is a good way to avoid spiritual practice. Silence and self-assuredness are therefore fruits that grow from the stalk of self-discipline, derived from the root of the Virtue of spiritual practice."

The disciple pleaded:

"Please speak further on the forth finger on the hand of Virtue, study of the Holy Books."

The sage said:

"The forth finger on the hand of Virtue is study of the Holy Books. To study the Holy Books is to read them, repeat them, and chant them endlessly. To study the Holy Books is to fill the spirit with holy thoughts. To not study the Holy Books is to fill the spirit with trash.

The Holy Books are like the polestar, guiding those along the Path towards the realization of the Supreme Self. Those who follow it through study will travel far on this Path. Those who do not follow it through not studying will become lost, forgetting even that there is a Path.

The Holy Books are like a tuning fork tuned to the note of Truth, bringing those in its proximity into resonance with its Truth. Those who hear it through study will resonate with its note in harmony. Those who do not hear it through not studying will not resonate with its note in disharmony.

To study the Holy Books is not to know their author, their date of authoring, or their history. To study the Holy Books is not to have a special edition thereof. To study the Holy Books is to read them repeatedly, to repeat them to yourself repeatedly, to memorize and chant them repeatedly. To study the Holy Books is to seek their Truth, know their Truth, and embody their Truth."

The disciple asked:

"Wise sage, are there any marks of one who practices the Virtue of study of the Holy Books?"

The sage replied:

"There is indeed a mark of one who practices the Virtue of study. Anyone who practices this Virtue will be focused. Whosoever practices this Virtue of study can see the Truths of the Holy Books hidden in all books and in all conversations; all words are brought into the focus of the Light of the Holy Books. Whosoever does not practice this Virtue is unfocused, being lead here and then there, around and around, without finding the Truth. Though a multitude of ideas may surround one who studies the Holy Books, he will always find the Truth therein. Though a multitude of ideas may surround one who does not study the Holy Books, he will never find Truth therein.

Whosoever studies the Holy Books studies themselves. Whosoever studies themselves studies the Holy Books. The Truth of the Holy Books is the Truth of the Self. The Truth of the Self is the Truth of the Holy Books. One who studies the Holy Books has focused their concentration, always remembering to accomplish the Great Work. One who does not study the Holy Books has not focused their concentration, always forgetting to accomplish the Great Work. Focus is therefore a mark of one who practices the Virtue of study of the Holy Books."

The disciple pleaded:

"Please speak further on the fifth finger on the hand of Virtue, self-surrender."

The sage said:

"The fifth finger on the hand of Virtue is self-surrender. [To practice the Virtue of self-surrender is to release attachment from the vain strivings of your ego in order to make room for the Lord within yourself, the Supreme Self.[45] To practice the Virtue of self-surrender is actually no surrender; to surrender falsity for Truth, weakness for Strength, partial for Complete: is that truly a surrender?

Self-surrender does not mean letting others dictate your life. Self-surrender does not mean flagellating and mortifying oneself. Self-surrender does not mean admitting to weakness. Self-surrender takes the greatest possible strength.

This surrender of the self is the offering of a sacrifice on the altar of the Lord. What kind of offering is a weak, lop-sided, and undeveloped self? What a great offering is the strong, balanced, and fully developed self! Therefore build up the self, feed it in body, mind, and spirit, for only thereby can this surrender be complete.[46]

One who practices the virtue of self-surrender says, 'It is not I but the Supreme Self who acts through me. It is not I but the Supreme Self who speaks through me. It is not I but the Supreme Self who thinks through me. Every thought, word, and deed of mine is a devotion to this Supreme Self. Every thought, word, and deed of others is a devotion to this Supreme Self. Every thought, word, and deed is this Supreme Self.'

One who does not practice the virtue of self-surrender says, 'I am I. I act for myself, yet no actions satisfy my body. I speak for myself, yet no words satisfy my mind. I think for myself, yet there is no Truth therein, and my spirit is never satisfied.'"

The disciple asked:

"Wise sage, are there any marks of one who practices the Virtue of self-surrender?"

The sage replied:

"There is indeed a mark of one who practices the Virtue of self-surrender. Anyone who practices this Virtue will be humble yet ever-active. Whosoever practices this Virtue of self-surrender accesses the omnipotence of the Supreme Self, becoming active and creative as he never could simply as himself. Though ever-active, he who practices this Virtue of self-surrender does not take credit for any of his creations, nor is attached to their success or failure.

One who practices the Virtue of self-surrender says, 'My feet dance this dance, but it is the Supreme Self who is the true mover of action, and therefore it is not my dance. My hands write this writing, but it is the Supreme Self who is the true thinker of thought, and therefore it is not my writing. My words speak this speech, but is the Supreme Self who is the true source of wisdom, and therefore it is not my speech.'

One who does not practice the Virtue of self-surrender takes credit for their action, their thought, and their wisdom. When their actions, words, and wisdom are praised, they are moved to happiness, and when their actions, words, and wisdom are criticized, they are moved to despair. [They are like a raft afloat at sea, buffeted and overturned by the waves of attraction and aversion.] One who practices the Virtue of self-surrender gives up clinging to the raft and thereby finds an island, unmoved by the buffeting waves of attraction and aversion. Constant activity and humility are therefore the marks of one who practices the Virtue of self-surrender.

Together, the five fingers of the hand of Control and the five fingers of the hand of Virtue constitute the Ten Disciplines. Together, they form the hands of greeting, of *namaste.* Together, they form the union of opposites, the realization of the Supreme Self."

The disciple bowed and began his practice.

AUMGN. AUMGN. AUMGN.

CHAPTER 7:
INNER KING UPANISHAD47

"The Perfect and the Perfect are one Perfect

and not two; nay, are none!"

–Liber AL vel Legis

All this is perfect. All that is perfect.

From perfection, perfection comes.

When perfection is taken from perfection,

Perfection still remains.

Horus, the Lord of Life and Love, is enshrined in the hearts of all and He pervades the whole universe. Called Ra-Hoor-Khuit, this Self is the supreme reality. Rejoice in Him by renouncing the sin of separateness.

Bind nothing! All belongs to this Lord of Infinite Space. Thus working with a pure will, you will live in eternal Light; thus Alone, one with your true Child-Self, you will work in true Liberty.

The Supreme Self is One.[48] He is the King of all kings, royal and ever-ready. Ever still, this true Self is swifter than thought, swifter than the senses. Though motionless, He outruns all pursuit. Without this Self, no life could exist. This Crowned and Conquering Self seems to move, but He is ever still; He seems far away, but is ever near. He is within all, and He transcends all.

Those who see all creatures in themselves and themselves in all creatures know neither fear nor pity. Those who see all creatures in themselves and themselves in all creatures know neither sorrow nor grief. How can the multiplicity of the world delude the one who abides in its unity?

Horus, the Supreme Self, is everywhere. Radiant is this Self: indivisible, untouched by sin, wise, both immanent and transcendent. It is He who holds the Cosmos together. It is He who *is* the Cosmos.[49]

The face of Truth is hidden by your orb of gold, O Sun! May you remove your orb so that I, who adore the True, may penetrate to your secret center and see the glory of Truth.[50] O Nourishing Sun – solitary traveler in the firmament, controller, hidden spring and source of Life for all things known and unknown – spread your Light and subdue your dazzling splendor so that I may see your blessed Self. Thou who art I beyond all I am: even that very Self am I!

May my life merge in the Immortal and Universal Life when my body is reduced to ashes. O mind, meditate on the eternal Hawk-Headed Lord of Love. O God of Force and Fire, lead us by the path of our True Wills to eternal joy, immanent and transcendent. Deliver us from good and from evil, we who Bind Nothing and drain our blood into the Cup of Babalon.

AUMGN. AUMGN. AUMGN.

CHAPTER 8:
SECRET OF DEATH UPANISHAD[51]

"This is the world of the waters of Maim;

this is the bitter water that becometh sweet.

Thou art beautiful and bitter, O golden one, O my Lord

Adonai, O thou Abyss of Sapphire! I follow Thee,

and the waters of Death fight strenuously against me.

I pass unto the Waters beyond Death and beyond Life."

–Liber Cordis Cincti Serpente

Once, long ago, Ta-Nech[52] gave away his possessions in order to obtain merit from the gods. He had a son named Ankh-af-na-khonsu[53] who, though only a young boy, had great understanding of and was filled with certainty about the Holy Books. Ta-Nech thought when the offerings were made:

"What merit is gained by giving away things that are too old to be used?"

Ankh-af-na-khonsu asked his father:

"To whom will you give me as an offering?"

Ankh-af-na-khonsu asked this repeatedly until Ta-Nech finally replied angrily:

"I give you to death!"

Ankh-af-na-khonsu then thought to himself:

> "I go in the midst of the many who are dying as the first of many who will die. I go on a mission to Osiris, the Lord of death. I see how it is with all those who came before: they all go to the land of death. I know how it will be with those who are living: they will also meet everyone else in death.[54] Like the crops ripen and then fall, and like the crops, they rise again and again."

Ankh-af-na-khonsu then traveled to the underworld in the West,[55] the Lord of death's abode, but Osiris was not there. He waited patiently for several days. When Osiris returned to his abode, he heard a voice saying:

> "When guests enter one's abode, they must be received well and with hospitality, given water to wash themselves. Those who are not hospitable to guests are far from wise, and they will lose all their hopes, all their accumulated merit."

Osiris then said:

"O noble guest, I grant you three wishes that I may atone for the inhospitable nights you have spent here."

Ankh-af-na-khonsu said:

"Lord of death, grant that my father's anger will cease, that he may recognize and receive me once I return with great love."

Osiris replied:

"I grant that Ta-Nech will love you. Once he sees you return from the maw of death, he will be at peace."

Ankh-af-na-khonsu then said:

"I have heard that there is no fear in the heavenly and Supernal abode, for there is no hunger, thirst, pain, or death. Everyone stands rejoicing in perpetuity in the kingdom of these Heavens.

I have also heard that you know the ritual of fire that leads to these Heavens. O Lord of the West, I have certainty in your wisdom and I ask for your instruction in this ritual. This is my second wish."

Osiris, the Lord of the West, taught Ankh-af-na-khonsu this fire ritual, how to erect an altar of fire in the heart, how to worship this fire as That from which the universe sprung and evolves. Ankh-af-na-khonsu learned these instructions quickly, and Osiris said:

"I grant you this necklace, formed of three interconnected rings. Those who have performed this ritual three times with utter sincerity and devotion, who have studied the Holy Books, performed their spiritual practices, and given away everything that is not devoted to the Great Work, who know their unity with father, mother, and the Supreme Self; unto them do I grant this gift. Knowing the fire in their hearts is the Deathless Sun, they rise above all death and attain the perfection of peace. Those who perform the triple duty of study, practice, and sacrifice, who perform this ritual of fire with full awareness of its inner meaning, they will lift the noose of death from their necks, they will transcend pain and sorrow, they will enter into the Heavens of pure joy.[56] What is your third wish?"

Ankh-af-na-khonsu stated:

"When a person dies, some people say, 'He still exists.' Others say, 'He no longer exists.' What is the truth?"

Osiris replied:

"This doubt haunts all the wise men and even the gods. The secret of death is difficult to understand. Ask me for some other wish, Ankh-af-na-khonsu, that I may fulfill my promise."

Ankh-af-na-khonsu said:

"This doubt haunts all the wise men and even the gods, as you say, O Lord of the West. I know I can be taught best by you and there is no wish that I have other than to learn the truth of the secret of death."

Osiris responded:

"Ask me for endless generations of healthy children. Ask for the lavish riches of the earth. Ask for long life or freedom from sickness. Ask to be the ruler of a great kingdom. Ask to have the perfect capacity to enjoy all pleasures of the earth. Ask for the most beautiful women, the most adorned chariots, the greatest skill in music, the greatest knowledge in sciences. Ask of me any of these things, but please do not ask me for the secret of death."

Ankh-af-na-khonsu insisted:

"All these pleasures do not last. All of these pleasures will pass with all the fleeting shadows of earth! Keep your healthy children, your lavish riches, your long life, women, chariots, skill, and knowledge. How can I be made satisfied by wealth while looking directly at your face?

Having approached a god as yourself, I ask how I can rejoice in a long life or in riches while I am still subject to old age and death? I seek only to know the secret of death. Therefore, dispel this doubt: Do people live or not live after death? I ask for nothing else than this secret of death."

Osiris was satisfied that Ankh-af-na-khonsu had passed all the tests given to separate the true aspirant from the false. Judging that the boy was fit to receive his secret, the Lord of the West slowly began to speak:

"The pure joy of the Supreme Self abides in all things forever, but not in what seems pleasant to the senses. Both the joy of the Supreme Self and the joy of the senses spur men to action, but they differ. [Whosoever chooses the joy of the Supreme Self will have perpetual well-being, but whosoever chooses the pleasures of the senses misses the Great Work of the goal of life.] A choice stands before all: eternal joy or fleeting pleasures? This is the choice one makes in all moments. It is only the wise who know there is a choice to make, whereas the ignorant and profane trod on in their ignorance. The wise accept what leads to pure joy even though it is painful to the senses at times. The ignorant run after fleeting pleasures, driven by their senses.

You are wise and have renounced these fleeting pleasures that the senses hold so dear, O Ankh-af-na-khonsu. You have turned your back on the ignorant way of the world that drives humanity to forget its ultimate goal in life. Wisdom and ignorance are galaxies apart. Wisdom leads to realization of the Supreme Self; ignorance leads to further and further estrangement from the True Self. This is why I regard you as worthy of this secret, O Ankh-af-na-khonsu, in that no fleeting pleasures tempt you to swerve from your holy Path.

Most men are ignorant even of their ignorance, yet they are wise in their own eyes. They are deluded, proud of the vanities of their learning, yet they go nowhere, walking round and round, like the blind leading the blind. They are mesmerized by the world of the senses, but the path to immortal Life lies beyond their sight. The ignorant believe, 'I am my body. When this body dies, I will die.' This is the superstitious faith they cling to, and because they live in this delusion, they fall under my sway life after life after life.

Only a few and secret hear about the Supreme Self. Fewer still dedicate their lives to the realization of this Supreme Self.

Praiseworthy and joyous is one who speaks about this Supreme Self. It is beyond rare to see those who make the realization of this Supreme Self their supreme goal of life.

The truth of the Supreme Self can never be divulged by anyone who has not realized that they are themselves the Supreme Self. The intellect cannot divulge the truth of the Supreme Self that lies beyond the duality of its subject and object. [Only those who see themselves in all beings, who see all beings in themselves, can help others to realize the Supreme Self for themselves.] This realization does not come through logic, nor does it come through scholarship. This realization comes only through earnest practice in the company of those who have realized this Truth and those who aspire unto it. You are wise, O Ankh-af-na-khonsu, because you seek this Supreme Self that is deathless and woundless.

Ankh-af-na-khonsu said:

"I know that all the pleasures of the senses, everything on earth, is fleeting like a shadow. I know that I can never reach the Deathless Sun through these fleeting delusions. This is why I have renounced all other desires but to attain the truth of the Supreme Self, and this is why I seek your instruction, Lord of the land of death."

Osiris continued:

⌈"Ankh-af-na-khonsu, I spread before your eyes the fulfillment of all earthly desires: The power to rule the earth, heavenly rewards gained through religious rites, miraculous spiritual powers beyond even time and space. These, with great wisdom and great Will, you have renounced.⌉

Realizing the timeless and immortal Self – That which is all perception yet hidden intimately in the chamber of the heart – the truly wise leave pain and pleasure far behind. Those who know they are, in truth, neither body nor mind but the Deathless and Supreme Self, the very divine principle of Life itself, find the source of all Joy, and they live and abide in pure and untarnished Joy. I see the gates of Joy are opening for you, Ankh-af-na-khonsu."

Ankh-af-na-khonsu pleaded:

"Teach me of That, which you see beyond right and wrong, good and evil, cause and effect, past and future!"

Osiris said:

"I will give you the holy Word that all the Holy Books are brilliant reflections thereof, that all spiritual disciplines strive towards and express. To attain this word, true aspirants lead a life of discipline, of action, senses, emotions, and thought, a life of self-emptying so that the True Self may shine through. This word is AUMGN. This immortal symbol of the Godhead is unsurpassed by all other words spoken by mankind. Realizing It, one finds complete fulfillment of all one's deepest strivings and longings. This Word is the greatest support and encouragement to all seekers of the Hidden Wisdom of the Deathless Self. Those in whose hearts AUMGN reverberates without ceasing, they are blessed and deeply loved as one who is united with the Supreme Self.

The all-encompassing Self was never born, and this all-embracing Self will never die. This Supreme Self is eternal, immutable, ineffable, beyond cause and effect, even beyond time and space. Beyond time, space, and causality, this True Self is one, individual, and eternal.[57] When the body ceases, the Self does not die.[58] When thoughts cease, the Self does not die. If the slayer believes that he can slay or the slain believes that he can be slain, neither knows the Truth of the

Self. This Deathless Self does not slay, nor is it ever slain; it cannot slay, nor can it ever be slain.[59]

Hidden in the heart of every man and every woman, even in the heart of all beings, the True Self abides.[60] This Self is both subtler than the subtlest and greater than the greatest. Those who give their last particle of dust[61] in the ecstasy of union[62] go beyond sorrow itself, they behold the glory of the Supreme Self through union with Horus, the Lord of Love.

[Though one sits in mediation in a particular place in space and time, the Self within exercises Its his influence at the farthest reaches of the universe. Though still, the Self moves everything everywhere.[63]]

When the wise realize this True Self that is without form in the midst of forms, without change in the midst of change, that is omnipresent, omnipotent, and supreme, they go beyond all shadows of sorrow.[64]

The True Self cannot be known through intellectual study of the Holy Books, nor through hearing discourses or lectures, nor through the intellect whatsoever. [The True Self can be attained only by those whom the Self chooses when they are enraptured in the union of meditation.] Yea, unto them that are enraptured in the union of meditation does the True Self reveal Itself.

This Supreme Self cannot be known by anyone who does not purify themselves from all profane actions, who does not control their senses, who does not still their mind, or who does not practice meditation. No one else but those who purify themselves of all profane actions, control their senses, still their minds, and practice meditation can know the omnipresent and omnipotent Self, whose radiant effulgence sweeps away the rituals of the magician, the words of the priest, the strength of the warrior, and It puts death itself to death, destroying even the Destroyer itself.[65]

[In the secret chamber of the heart in the temple of our bodies, two are seated by the fountain of Life. The separate ego drinks of the sweet and bitter water, liking the sweet, disliking the bitter, while the Supreme Self drinks sweet and bitter neither liking this nor disliking that.] The ego gropes in darkness, while the Self lives in Light. This is what all illumined sages and masters have declared, those who worship the sacred Flame in the name of the Lord of Light, Life, and Love.

[May we light the sacred Fire, Ankh-af-na-khonsu, that disintegrates the separate ego, enabling us to pass from the fear-embroiled world of fragmentation into the utterly fearless fullness of the changeless, deathless Whole.]

Know the Supreme Self as Lord of the chariot, the body as the chariot itself, the True Will as charioteer, and the disciplined mind as the reins. [The senses and passions are the horses that drive the chariot, and the universe is the road they travel.]

When we confuse the Self with the body, the senses, the mind, and thoughts, the Self appears to enjoy pleasure and suffer pain. When one lacks Wisdom, when the body and mind are undisciplined, the senses and thoughts run to and fro like wild and untamed horses. Even so, these horses obey the reins like trained horses when one has the Wisdom of Will and sharpened the mind through discipline to become one-pointed. Those who lack this Wisdom, confusing the Self with the ego, having little control over their senses and thoughts, distant from true purity of Will, never reach the pure joy of eternal Life but wander from day to night. Even so, those who have this Wisdom of Will, those with disciplined senses and a still mind, will reach the end of the journey, never falling into the pit of death again. With the Will as charioteer and the disciplined mind as reins, these wise ones will attain the supreme goal of life, the *Summum Bonum*, the Great Work of becoming united with the secret Lord of Light, Life, Love, and Liberty.[66]

Sensory stimuli and the sensory faculties derive from the world of the senses[67], the world of senses derive from sense-perception, sense-perception derives from mind, mind derives from ego, ego derives from undifferentiated consciousness, and undifferentiated consciousness derives from the Supreme Self.

This Supreme Self is the first cause and last effect. Horus, the Supreme Lord of Light, the hidden Self in every being,[68] does not shine forth. The light is merely Its reflection. The Supreme Self is revealed only to those who keep their concentration one-pointed on the Lord of Love and thus develop a super-conscious way of knowing.[69]

[Meditation enables them to go deeper and deeper into consciousness, from the world of sense to the world of words, from the world of words to the world of thoughts, and then beyond thoughts to Hidden Wisdom of the Supreme Self.]

Rise up! Awake![70] Seek the guidance of truly illumined masters, and realize the Supreme Self! The wise say this path is like a razor's edge, immeasurably difficult to traverse.

This Supreme Self is beyond all names[71] and beyond all forms, beyond the senses, beyond the mind, immutable, ineffable, inexhaustible, without beginning, without end, beyond time, space, and causality. Those who realize the Supreme Self are forever free from birth and death, forever free from pain and sorrow.

Only the wise who gain direct and experiential knowledge[72] attain the wisdom, understanding, and beauty[73] of living in super-conscious awareness of Truth. Only those who are filled with the fire of devotion, reciting the supreme Word of AUMGN, whether alone or among other spiritual seekers, are fit for the direct knowledge of eternal Life. Yea, only they are indeed fit for eternal Life.

The self-existent, self-created, self-perpetuated Lord of Life pierced the Veil of duality, entering the senses of the body to turn outward and see the world of multiplicity. Thus we look to the world outside and do not ever see the Supreme Self abiding within us. The wise withdraw their attachment to the senses, non-attached to the world of change, seek the principle of immortality itself, and look within: only then do they behold the Deathless Self.

It is only the immature that run after the pleasures of senses and run away from the pains of senses, inevitably falling into the ever-present trap of death and sorrow. [Only the wise, knowing the Supreme Self as eternal, never seek the Immutable in the world of mutability, never seek the Changeless in the world of change.]

It is the Supreme Self through which one truly enjoys shapes of the eye, tastes of the tongue, smells of the nose, sounds of the ear, feelings of the body, and sexual union of the generative organs. How can there possibly be anything unknown to That who is the One in many, the None in All? Know the indivisible One, and you will therefore know the All. It is the Supreme Self through which one enjoys waking consciousness and dream consciousness. To know That, the Supreme and Deathless Self, the undifferentiated and unitive consciousness, is to go beyond change, beyond sorrow, and beyond death itself.

The wise go beyond all fear when they know the Supreme Self as the true enjoyer of the fruit of the vine of the senses, for this Self is supreme!

Isis, the Lady of all birth and creation, born of the Supreme Godhead before even the formless and dark waters of the universe were created,[74] abides in the heart of all beings. Even She is the Self, for this Self is supreme!

Tahuti, the Lord of all energy and motion and magick, born of the Supreme Godhead through Its vital Life-force, father of all the forces of the cosmos, abides in the heart of all beings, at the Center of the Cross of the Elements. Even He is the Self, for this Self is supreme!

Even I, Osiris, the Lord of all death, born of the Supreme Godhead through Its fermentation, ever-present even in the Womb of Isis and the Life-Rod of Tahuti, abide in the heart of all beings. Even I, Lord of the West, is the Self, for this Self is Supreme!

That which is the source of all forms, the source of all forces, the center and secret of the Sun itself,[75] beyond which there is no birth nor death, no coming nor going, no cause nor effect, is the Self, for this Self is supreme!

What you see here is also there, and what you see as there is also here: whosoever sees only multiplicity but not the One, indivisible, unconquerable Self must wander on and on from day to day, from night to night, from death to death.

Only the one-pointed concentration of mind attains this unitive state of pure joy. In Truth, there is no one but the Supreme Self. Whosoever sees multiplicity but not the One, indivisible, unconquerable Self must wander on and on from day to day, from night to night, from death to death.

That unextended point enshrined in the heart,[76] ruler of time, past, present, and future, of which we go beyond all fear and sorrow when we perceive It... That is indeed the Self, for this Self is supreme!

That unextended point, a flame without smoke, an omnipresent center without circumference, ruler of time, past and present and future, changeless on this day as yesterday and as tomorrow... That is indeed the Self, for this Self is supreme!

As the rain on the apex of a pyramid runs off the the slopes on all sides, so those who only perceive the multiplicity of the world run after pleasures and run away from pains on all sides. As pure water poured into pure water becomes the very same essence, so does the self of every illumined man or woman become one with the Supreme Self, the Deathless Godhead of Eternity!

There is a palace with four gates of which the ruler is the unborn and undying Self.[77] This Self is a Sun whose Light shines forever. The wise who meditate on this Supreme Self go beyond sorrow, they are freed from the ever-turning wheel of activity, sloth, and balance, the wheel of birth, life, and death, for this Self is supreme![78]

The Self is the Sun shining in the heavens, the wind blowing in space, the water lying on the breast of earth,[79] the fire in the hearth, and the guest in the home. This Self dwells in the heart of all beings, in all gods, in all truth, in all the vast expanse of the heavenly firmament. This Self is the gnomes of earth, the sylphs of air, the undines of water, and the salamanders of fire[80]; this Self pervades all, for this Self is supreme!

The Supreme Beloved who abides in the heart rules the breath of life.[81] We live not by the breath that flows in and flows out, but by That who causes the breath to flow in and flow out. All five senses pay their homage to this Self, and all thoughts pay their homage to this Self. When the Dweller in the body is released from the body, mind, and all shadows of the earth, what remains?[82] The Self, for this Self is supreme!

Now, O Ankh-af-na-khonsu, I will tell you of this unseen, intangible, eternal Self,[83] and what happens to the individual after death. Those who are unaware of this Supreme Self are transmuted into other forms. That which is awake even in our sleep, giving shape to the objects of sense-cravings in dreams, That indeed is pure Joy, pure Light, Horus the Immortal Sun, whose body is the Tree of Life itself,[84] and beyond whom none can go... for this Self is supreme!

As fire takes different shapes when it consumes objects of different shape, so does the One Self take the shape of all things in which It is present. As the air assumes different shapes when it enters objects of different shape, so does the One Self take the shape of all things in which It is present.

As the Sun, the eye of the world, cannot be tainted by the defects in our eyes or by the objects it shines upon, so the One Self, dwelling in all, cannot be tainted by the shadows of the world: this Self transcends all, for this Self is supreme!

The Supreme Ruler, the inner Self of all things, multiplies Its Oneness into the many.[85] Pure and eternal Joy is theirs who see the Self in their own hearts, and to no one else does it ever come!

Immutable amidst the mutable, Changeless amidst the things that pass away,[86] pure Joy in all who are truly conscious, the One answers the devotional aspiration of many. Perfect peace is theirs who see the Self in their own hearts, and to no one else does it ever come!"

Ankh-af-na-khonsu asked:

"How can I know that Supreme and Ineffable Self that is realized by the wise? Is It the Light itself or does It reflect Light?"

Osiris replied:

"In the Self, there shines not the Sun, neither Moon nor star shine, nor lightning-flash nor fire lit on earth shine at all. [The Self is the True Light reflected by all. It is always shining, and everything shines as a reflection of It.]

The Tree of Eternity has its roots above in the One and its branches on earth below in the many.[87] Its pure root is Supreme Self, the Immortal from whom all the worlds draw their light and life, whom none can transcend, for this Self is supreme!

The entire universe comes forth from this Supreme Self and moves in It. With Its power, the universe reverberates like thunder crashing in the heavens. Those who realize this Deathless Self pass beyond the grips of death.

In holy awe of It, fire burns; in holy awe of It, the Sun shines, the clouds rain, and the winds blow. In holy awe of It, death stalks about the gates and by-ways of life to kill.

If one fails to realize the Supreme Self in this life before the body dissolves, countless other forms will be embodied until the world of multiplicity is transcended.

The Supreme Self can be seen in the pure heart as if in a mirror; it can be seen with a pure heart in a dream, in the reflections of trembling waters, in the clear light of the subtle worlds.

The wise do not grieve, for they know they do not confuse the senses with the Self, they know that all sense experience is fleeting. The senses depend on the mind, the mind on consciousness, the consciousness on ego, and above the ego is the First Cause. Beyond even the First Cause of the universe is the Supreme Self, omnipresent, omnipotent, omniscient, ineffable, beyond time, beyond space, beyond causality, beyond all names, beyond all forms, beyond all attributes. Realizing the Supreme Self, one is released from the cycle of birth and death, from past and future, from pain and pleasure, from all things in the realm of multiplicity.

The Supreme Self is formless: It can never be seen with these two eyes, but It reveals Itself in the heart made pure through discipline of the senses and emotions and the focus of the mind in meditation. Realizing the Supreme Self, one is released from the cycle of birth and death, from past and future, from pain and pleasure, from all things in the realm of multiplicity.

When the five senses are stilled, when emotions are stilled, when thoughts are stilled: this is called the highest state by the wise. They say that true Union, true Love, is this complete and utter Silence in which one enters the unitive state, never to become confused with the separate and multiple again. The sense of unity will come and go if one is not well-established in this state.

This Supreme Self is attained through the unitive state. This state of total Union cannot be attained through words, through reading, through hearing, through sights, sounds, smells, tastes, or even through thoughts. How can it be attained except through one who is established in this state through pure, consistent, and earnest meditation?

There are two selves: the separate ego and the Indivisible Self. When one rises above 'I, me, mine' in meditation, the Supreme Self is revealed as one's real self.

When all the petty desires, wishes, and whims that surge and course through our heart are understood and renounced for the Great Work itself, the temporal becomes eternal, the mortal becomes immortal, the death-embroiled becomes death-transcendent. There are hundreds of tracks that emanate from the heart, the many desires, wishes, and whims. Only one leads to the crown of the head, the True Will: this way leads to immortality and the rest lead to death. When all the knots, skeins, and veins that tangle and strangle the heart are loosened in meditation, the temporal becomes eternal, the mortal becomes immortal, the death-embroiled becomes death-transcendent. This is the sum total of all the Holy Books. Rise up! Awake! Attain to the realization of one's self as the Supreme Self!

The Lord of Love, an unextended point, is ever abiding and ever enshrined in the hearts of all beings. Draw out this Lord within oneself through meditation: still the senses, still the emotions, still the mind: Know thy Self to be pure, immortal, ever-conquering, ever-joyful! Know thy Self to be pure, immortal, ever-conquering, ever-joyful!"

Ankh-af-na-khonsu learned from the Lord of Death the discipline of meditation. Liberating himself from the shadow of separateness, Ankh-af-na-khonsu won immortality in the Supreme Self. Everyone is likewise blessed who knows this Supreme Self.

AUMGN. AUMGN. AUMGN.

CHAPTER 9:
GREAT WORD UPANISHAD88

"Aum! let it fill me!

The light is mine;

its rays consume me."

–Liber AL vel Legis

Let us meditate on the Great Word – AUMGN – the Word that issued at the Dawn of the Universe and reverberates in the hearts of all beings.[89]

AUMGN stands for the Supreme Reality. It is a symbol for what was, and is, and is to come.[90] AUMGN is also what abides beyond past, present, and future.

Horus is all, and the Self is Horus. The name of this Self is Horus and his Word is Will. The Will is Silence and Speech. When it speaks, it is the Word: AUMGN.

The Word AUMGN arises out of Silence, the Nothing beyond the three dimensions of Space, beyond the arrow of Time, beyond the binding links of causality.[91] In this Silence, countenance beholds not countenance, beauty answers not beauty.[92] There is no thing distinguished from any other thing in this Silence,[93] yet All abides as a seed in soil, waiting to sprout into the Bodhi-Tree at the axis of the World,[94] as a babe in an egg waiting to spring crowned and conquering from the womb.[95] There is speech unspoken in this Silence.[96]

Out of this Silence, there comes the Word: AUMGN.[97]

First, the sound "A" vibrates as a Beginning. The first of the letters; it emerges from deep in the throat; it is the Breath of Life, the cry of Birth.[98] "A" resounds as a First, and thereby it implies a Last; it is a Beginning warranting an inevitable End.[99] Like the Solar Priest emerging spotless and pure as a fool from the Tomb in the Beginning, he must thereby surely return thereto in the End.[100] This is the wrath of the Word that things are thus; this is the grace of the Word that things are thus.[101] This is the Mystery of Sin justified by the Mystery of Redemption; this is the Mystery of Separation justified by the Mystery of Union.[102]

From this, the sound becomes "U," directed and restrained, and this discipline is sustenance.[103] It is the booming roar of the Lion, the Sun's far-darting rays at the pinnacle of its power.[104] This sound is the maturation into Adulthood, the acquisition of the Hierophant's elevenfold staff amidst the balance of the Four Powers and Elements within oneself.[105] By this sound we shine as little suns, giving out Light and Life;[106] by this sound we unite strength and skill in love under will;[107] by this sound we gaze upon the world and see the multitudinous Beauty of its multiplicity and the seal of Unity therein.[108]

From this, the mouth begins to close; the breath begins to expire; the Word is almost exhausted. The lips come together as a seal, resounding with the sound "M": the sound of Water, of Death, of the Mother;[109] the sound of satisfaction after a meal; the sound of the last rays of fading Light.[110] Favorable is this sound to those who face it standing upright, heads erect, and eyes open.[111] Those who fear it will not hear the subtle shift as the "M" becomes "GN."

The course of Breath is finished, yet there is that which remains. "GN" is the sound of Gnosis, the knowledge beyond mere mind, the certainty of the Life that transcends the endless undulations of the serpent's slither through systole and diastole, through birth and death, through speech and silence; it *is* the Serpent, the Wisdom of Immortal Life itself, crowning those with the Gnosis of this True, Mighty, Deathless, Woundless Self.[112] GN is the Light passed from mouth to ear, from heart to heart, from generation unto generation, persisting through yet transcending the rise and fall of nations, the turning of the seasons, the days and nights.[113] It is the superconscious state, neither inward nor outward, beyond the senses and reason, where there is none other than the Supreme Self, the ultimate goal of life, source of infinite peace, infinite light, and infinite love.[114] Realize Him!

GN is the sound of Generation, the procreative Life-Will that expresses itself in All,[115] and perpetuates itself through Love; it is the power to transform – to beget and to destroy[116] – the casting of a stone into the sea, creating endlessly reverberating ripples throughout all space and all time. It is the axle of the Wheel, sending out spokes to manifest the Word, yet abiding unchanged, unmoved, unscathed, ever in the center.[117] It is the Sun, ever-shining though it appears to rise and fall; it is the Moon, ever-guiding the tides of life though She appears to wax and wane; it is the Earth, ever-moving but still in Space. It is the Supreme State, without parts, beyond birth, beyond death, a symbol of pure and everlasting joy. GN is the sound that abides in Silence. Listen closer: a mighty swelling of force will be heard; a deep, deep drone of the beetle,[118] the influx of the Breath of Spirit for the Word to be sounded and sung once more, a million times more, innumerable times upon innumerable times more, all for the glory of All, all for the joy of Naught. Those who know AUMGN as the Self become the Self; truly, they become the Self. Let us meditate upon the Great Word:

AUMGN. AUMGN. AUMGN.

An Incredibly Long Interlude:

The Lost Sutra of Harold

INTRODUCTION
BY OMNISCIENT NARRATOR

If omniscience is a characteristic of divinity, I cannot imagine how She bears this burden with such carefree delicacy. I would trade it for mere multiscience any day of the week, for omniscience curses one with the knowledge not only of all truth but all falsehood as well. To peer into the porous channels of Harold's brain, one must withstand much falsehood, indeed. I will not even deign to describe what I have discerned within *you*, dear reader.

Despite what misgivings I may have in relating this tale to my readers, I can unhesitatingly swear that everything here written actually happened. Certain, and most true.[119] That is, thoughts occurred that lead to their being put onto these pages. That these words are written are evidence that they were thought; that they were thought is evidence of their having happened. They have happened and, with your most noble assistance, they will happen again for a second showing in your mind's theater. Being omniscient, I am fully aware that this demonstration is not particularly convincing. Unfortunately for you, most dear reader, I never claimed to be omnibenevolent.

Since both Harold and myself have a weakness for witticism, and I – containing all knowledge of past, present, and future in my dissociated database – have foreseen that many of the more obscure, cheap, coarse, or crude allusions, implications, and references may pass uncomprehended, unnoticed, unexposed, unappreciated, and many another un-words.[120] Therefore, in my wisdom and unparalleled foresight, I have appended several notes at the end of this tome. If it be your style to want to know the various references being made and you happen to enjoy flipping back and forth incessantly, this effort will not have been in vain. If it be your style to read undistracted or to generally blunder through books, then I understand, though I do not necessarily hold your choice in high regard. Regardless of your decision, if you proceed any further, I foresee great laughterful caresses of nihilistic absurdity in your near future.[121]

Though I know all things, I still cannot seem to understand my own motives in deciding to put down this story in material form. Your motives in taking time out of your brief blip of a life on this space-rock are even more unclear yet. Some things, it seems, remain unknowable and one must simply accept them. Therefore, I hope you will join me and Kierkegaard[122] at the edge of this cliff, and take a leap of faith into Harold's world.

The most knowledgable storyteller that the publisher could afford,

Omniscient Narrator

PART 1:

THE BURSTING-FORTH OF HAROLD FROM THE GREAT WOMB OF TIME

"Life does not cease to be funny when people die
any more than it ceases to be serious when people laugh."
–George Bernard Shaw

Harold was a good fetus: healthy, happy, content. He might have fashioned himself the anti-Jonah[123] – willingly enveloped in the dark but warm caverns of the great maternal whale-belly – if it weren't for the fact that subject and object were not yet distinguished in his world-awareness. For now, he was a veritable Harpocrates,[124] giving the eternal Sign of Silence in that unmanifest state of pure potentiality. Yet this eternal now had a paradoxically abrupt end.

No one seems to discuss how utterly messy the incarnation of a God into Matter really can be. Salty blood spewed from the averse mouth of the mother, basking the sterile hospital accroutements in a thick film of birth-refuse. It is said that a Buddha can be identified by certain oddities of the infant's body upon birth. No one knows who said it, but someone, somewhere, at some point, certainly said something similar. When Harold popped head-first out of the Great

Womb of Time,[125] birthed from black eternity into the light of limitation, he seemed to give a sacred mudra to the wise men gathered about the birth-table: the fingers of his right hand were clenched except for the medius, which was extended with force and grace into the air as if to say in response to his birth, "This insult has not gone unnoticed." It was almost as if Harold, from the moment of exiting the tight quarters of his nine-month confinement, determined to enter upon that great Path of Return[126] back into the womb. Freud would certainly be proud.

Harold gasped for air, choked on his own cries, and then a bellow burst forth from his bowels. The sacred sound emitted from the flapping vocal chords of his buttocks, announcing the coming of the Lord like the blowing of the ram's horn by the Hebrew high priest.[127] He had just exited the holy tabernacle, having been himself the Ark of the Covenant, the hallowed symbol of the covenant of God and beast mixed into one.[128]

Harold's throat cleared and he cried as most infants do, but the doctors stood back slightly astonished. The infant's cry sounded like a death-rattle: his bloody film was his death-jacket, his umbilical cord was his noose. Harold was alive, but the first moments of life seemed to be spent in symbolic acknowledgment of his inevitable death. Already, he had grasped the immortal truth of mortality, the unchangeable fact of his changeability.

"An evil omen," one doctor muttered.

"Nonsense, it is a portend of a savior!" another doctor cried.

"I think I pooped a little," whimpered the mother.

Thus entereth Harold into the Abyss of Consciousness.

PART 2:

FROM THE MOUTH OF BABES[129]
COMES A LOT OF NONSENSE

"Reality is merely an illusion, albeit a very persistent one."
–Albert Einstein

"Consider the color green," Harold commented to a group of peers gathered at his feet. Harold swept his hand through the air in a grand gesture, "It surrounds us, it binds us, it bursts from the very ground upon which we walk!" The group nodded in agreement, enraptured by the impassioned plea to partake in that rarest of all human qualities: deep thinking.

"We all agree upon the green-ness of this green," Harold continued while plucking out a few pieces of grass from the ground, "yet consider this: Perhaps what I see as green, you see as red!" He pointed viciously at a person perched in front of the crowd, who was taken aback with a gasp. "Perhaps what I see as green, you see as blue!" The entire crowd Ooh'ed and Aah'ed in amazement at these divine truths. "It may be that you may even see the entire world in a blend of colors of which I have never nor will ever perceive!" The crowd furrowed their brows simultaneously in the fruitless endeavor of attempting to imagine a color they had never perceived before.

"'Green!' we say, 'green!' We all use the same word, but how do we know we all are talking about the same color? I demand an answer!" After a brief pause, one fearless explorer of philosophy raised her hand. "Yes, my dear? Do you know the answer?" Harold questioned in an almost sarcastic condescension.

"I believe the answer is that we don't know," she replied with a rare blend of timidity and confidence.

"Indeed, we *don't* know! Not only this, but I have learned from a reliable source that what we perceive as green is exactly what it is not. We see by means of light, which bounces off this grass and enters into our eyeballs. The nature of the light that bounces off carries the message of 'green' to our brains, yet consider this as well! If green-ness is exactly what is reflected off of the grass, it has absorbed all other colors: it is everything *except* green! What we see is exactly what is not!" The crowd gasped in horror – Harold thought he could hear mutters of "the world is a lie" and even a "God is dead!"[130]

"Yes, troubling isn't it? We can't even agree upon the color of grass! Not only can we never agree upon the simplest thing as to the color of grass, we are blinded by our use of the same term to describe it. Not only this, but our very perception of the grass is more than an illusion – it is an outright lie! We must all write to our

Congresspeople and declare that free speech has gone too far! We the people demand that grass tell our brains the truth! We demand to see reality, not the inverted cloak that we have heretofore called 'awareness!' In the name of freedom, in the name of reality, in the name of Truth! Down with tyranny! Down with illusion! Down with ignorance! To arms, my brothers and sisters, to arms!"

The outbreak of battle-cries amongst the people was cut short by the bell clanging its repetitive and abrasive song across the field. Recess was over, and all the children followed Harold back into the preschool.

Thus preacheth Harold to the people.

PART 3:

THE PRECEPTS[131] AND PERCEPTS OF A LONELY PEDESTRIAN UPON THE PATH OF PERFECTION

"Prisons are built with stones of Law,
Brothels with bricks of Religion."
−William Blake

When Harold crossed the Rubicon[132] of thirteen years old, he became a Buddhist. While he joined no monastery and wore clothes that made him indistinguishable from any other pedestrian on the streets, he was a fan of numbered lists and so the allure of Buddhism was inescapable. He was, after all, known to be prone to bouts of spiritual impulsivity.

Harold was absolutely certain of the Three Characteristics of existence – everything contained suffering, everything was impermanent, nothing had a substantial self. He was utterly convinced of the necessity of the Three Refuges of Buddha, Dharma, and Sangha, and he firmly believed the Four Noble Truths were the only logical conclusions to any rudimentary analysis of the nature of the world.[133] The Five Precepts, on the other hand, did not interest Harold. They actually seemed to him to be cruel jokes played by the Buddha upon the weak-minded rabble who were too stupid to see through them.

"I cannot abstain from taking life unless I stop breathing so that I might not unintentionally inhale microscopic lifeforms, in which case I would be shortly taking my own life," Harold explained to a man at a bus stop.

"I cannot abstain from stealing because there are no substantial selves with which to posses other substantial objects," he continued. "I cannot abstain from sensuality and sexual conduct because I have just hit puberty, and I am convinced that the forces of hormones rival that of gravity. Further, adultery implies possession and I cannot begin to believe that there can ever be property in human flesh except through the machinations of that most insidious human abortion known as the Court." Harold started to pace around the man, swinging his limbs about to exaggerate his points. "I cannot abstain from false speech because words and names are the foremost of all lies, attributing solidity to that which is, by its nature, impermanent and ever-changing."

The bus then arrived and the man got on quickly, not having understood a word of what Harold was describing since he didn't speak English. Harold didn't seem to notice or care and continued his diatribe while pacing excitedly, "I cannot abstain from intoxication unless it so be that I remove all senses, for they all distort perception as much as alcohol – even worse, because we don't count ourselves 'drunk' when imbibing sights and sounds and all the rest! The Two Truths doctrine, the Three Characteristics, the Three Refuges, the Four Noble Truths, the Five Aggregates, the Six Senses, the Seven Factors of Enlightenment, the Eightfold Path, the Nine Yanas, the Ten Perfections, the Twelve Links of Dependent Origination, the Fourteen Unanswerable Questions[134]... I accept all of these, but I can never accept the Five Precepts!" At the culmination of his paean, Harold took off his sandals, placed them on his head, and walked away. The bench at the bus stop then spontaneously achieved enlightenment.[135]

Thus initiateth Harold the bench of Bodhisattva Boulevard.

PART 4:

THE INEXORABLE MUTABILITY OF PHENOMENA, OR HOW HAROLD ACHIEVED THE GRADE OF $2°=9^{\square}$[136]

*"When your child comes down the stairs, this is the First Moment all
over again; this is Buddha meeting Buddha over toast, over milk,
over mu tea & coffee & porridge & brown rice.
We never had breakfast before!"*
–Baba Ram Dass

At some point, Harold lost his sandals so he was forced to
walk barefoot through suburbia. He came upon a childhood friend's
house and knocked on the door three times.

"Who is it?" came a voice from inside. Harold knocked five
more times.

"Who's there?" the concealed voice said a bit louder. Harold
knocked three final times,[137] and the door swung open. "Goddamnit,
Harold. You only have to knock once."

"I must have picked up a certain Masonic breed of OCD on
my way here," Harold confessed. "May I come inside and perhaps
borrow some shoes?"

"Of course." The friend stepped back and motioned to show Harold inside. Upon entering, Harold felt a heavy darkness in the house.

Harold inquired, "Have you been meddling with the Goetia, my brother?"[138]

"I work with demons every day, but not of the Goetic breed," the friend replied, for he worked in the IT field. Harold began to chuckle to himself. His chuckle slowly broke into a heaving guffaw and his friend turned to him, "Have you gone more mad than usual?"

"I have found that laughter is the best banishing," Harold replied. His attention turned to the kitchen sink, where a brittle pyramid of dirty dishes lay since ancient times. "In return for your hospitality, may I wash your dishes?"

"Whatever floats your boat, I guess," the friend conceded.

"My boat floats on the firmament in the car called Millions-of-Years!"[139] Harold exclaimed.

"Yeah, OK, just don't break anything."

Harold shuffled to the sink and began to wash the dishes. The laughter also had the unintended side-effect of loosening the girders of his soul.[140] As Harold scrubbed, the veil of illusory solidity washed away. He looked at the dishes and thought to himself, "A bunch of dirty dishes piled up at random is the most beautifully noble structure ever created[141] – who would ever say it is unclean or in need of tidying?" Harold then lifted his head and glanced out the window to the pool outside. A deck chair that he had once sat in a year or so ago caught his eye, and he immediately put down the spoon and sponge in his hands to investigate further. Concerned about the welfare of his patio furniture, the friend followed him outside.

Harold stopped next to the deck chair and turned to his friend. He remarked, "The meeting of an object like this deck chair at some point in the future illustrates the futility of all attachment." Without letting his friend respond, Harold turned back to the deck chair and offered a greeting.

"Hello, chair, you aren't quite the same as I remembered you." A seemingly eternal moment passed. "...Nor am I quite the same either," he confessed. "In fact, it seems we are two strangers meeting for the first time... although memory insists otherwise!"

"What in Geb's name are you blathering about?"[142] the friend asked in mild desperation.

"*Panta rhei*, brother.[143] I am not who I am.[144] Nor are you, so each moment we spend together we must introduce ourselves anew. Nothing lasts, but nothing is lost."[145]

"Why, then, nothing would have solidity!" the friend complained, "Nothing would be worthwhile; there would be no action or goal that was justifiable! God save us!"

"God? I have no need of that hypothesis," Harold said while channeling LaPlace.[146] "Besides, the world is only justifiable as an aesthetic phenomenon.[147] Everything that is, is enough.[148] Sit back and enjoy the show, then!" Harold then turned, walked through the house, and back onto the street, having forgotten why the 5-minutes-ago-Harold went there in the first place.

Thus solveth Harold the paradox of Motion and Rest.

PART 5:

THE TAVERN OF SPIRITUAL INTOXICATION, AND HOW HAROLD FORSAKED BUDDHISM

"All this talk about 'suffering humanity' is principally drivel
based on the error of transferring one's own psychology
to one's neighbour... It is necessary that we stop, once and for all,
this ignorant meddling with other people's business.
Each individual must be left free to follow his own path."
–Aleister Crowley

Harold then picked up his head and realized he was alone, but his feet had led him to the threshold of a bar called the Motley Cow.[149] He caught a glimpse of an attractive, young lady entering the bar and immediately determined to break the third and fifth Precepts as soon as possible.[150] He passed by some picketers who claimed that alcohol was mortal sin that condemned one's soul to eternal torment and approached the tavern.

Upon arriving at the entrance, Harold was confronted by the ever-looming Dweller on the Threshold.[151] "Got your ID?" he asked.

Harold said, "I may look young, but that is because my inner child helplessly shines through my pores. This inner child, though, has an inner cantankerous grandma who, I assure you, is quite authentic: she smells of mothballs and Maltomeal." Harold flashed his fake ID after flashing his wit, and the Dweller let him pass into the tavern, for Harold knew the most worthwhile weapons against authority were confusion and confidence.

Harold glanced around and saw the basic buffoonery one would expect within a place with such a ridiculous name. College students drunkenly drowned themselves in debauch, throwing themselves headlong into the hopeless Hunt, destined for destruction regardless of how many wingmen guided their ways.

The sights saddened Harold who exclaimed, "Oh, pitiful sorrow! Oh, wretched existence! Oh, cacophanous babbling of blind creatures!" For he was wont to confuse the promptings of his irritable bowels for pangs of conscience. All of the relentless pleasure-seeking put a bad taste in Harold's mouth. He considered all the pub-crawlers to be miserable maggots feasting upon their own livelihoods. Harold lamented, "Some men are born posthumously, but it seems many are prehumously dead!"[152] He shook his head dramatically, perching his brow delicately upon his forefinger and thumb before throwing his head back and outward to exclaim, "It seems no one has even begun to grasp that First, most Noble Truth! Is there no hope for humanity? Is there no help for the widow's son!?"[153]

In the grips of despair, tumbling down the tunnel of tumultuous desperation, Harold caught hold of a crag of cherubic comprehension. He realized his irreparable error: it was *he* who was sorrowful, not those who tumbled about the tables! In a flash, his Buddhism was seen as nothing more than typical teenage angst, sublimated onto the plane of spirituality. Harold grabbed a nearby imbiber by the collar and shook him, "Mea culpa! Mea culpa! Mea maxima culpa!"[154]

Harold spun on his heel and the entire Motley Cow was transformed into the Heavenly Hathor. The bar-goers were saints whose intoxication was spiritual ecstasy. The bartender was the very Hierophant of the Mysteries, distributing the draught of divine gnosis. Those who stood outside with signs of sin were purse-proud yet ultimately penniless[155]: they were puffed up with the flatulent air of falsity. "The next round is on me!" Harold proclaimed triumphantly. Everyone cheered, and in the excitement, Harold slipped away since he had forgotten to go to an ATM.

Thus exiteth Harold from the path of renunciation.

PART 6:

THE IRONIES OF ISIS, OR THE UNCOVERING OF THE CONTRADICTION KNOWN AS MAN

"Everybody gets so much information all day long
that they lose their common sense."
–Gertrude Stein

After exiting his Buddhist self-(and-world-)loathing, Harold entered a movie theater and saw a screening of *The Matrix*, so he began to fancy himself a philosopher. Like all philosophers, he engaged in that vain endeavor to lift the veil of Nature to see Her true essence.[156]

At first, Harold agreed with Thales that the world is of the nature of water, for everything finds its level and sinks to conform to the lowest crevice or common denominator. Democracy was irrefutable evidence of this. Upon hearing Heraclitus, he switched to believe that the world is of the nature of fire, for everything is constantly burning, exchanging its form for another. Fashion was irrefutable evidence of that, for it is a form of ugliness so unbearable it must be altered every season.[157] Abruptly, he assented to Anaximenes that air must be the answer, for it is air that permeates all things, sometimes compressed and sometimes uncompressed, going in through the top and out through the bottom. The fact that it allowed for a fart joke assured Harold of its authenticity. He then renounced rationality and embarked on the empirical enterprise, asserting that all things are earthly and the appearance otherwise is but a material mirage. Having spoken with many people, Harold found no evidence of these mysterious things called "minds."

After these few minutes of meditation, Harold decided that none of these answers were truly satisfying, and he decided that metaphysics were merely misinterpreted metaphors. Having disabused himself of such speculation, he went for a walk and came upon a supermarket where hippies were protesting the corporate encroachment upon their hometown.

"Humanity has sown the seeds of its own destruction!" preached one of the hairiest hippies.

"We have become corrupt!" another chimed in. "We have turned our backs on Mother Nature! She will take her revenge!"

"We have lost our tribal roots," the first hippie said even louder than before, for he was most interested in looking like a prophet. "Down with corporate America! Up with communes! We must return to Nature!"

"Yes!" Harold cried sarcastically, getting the hippies' attention. "Repent, all ye sinners! The day of the Goddess'

Judgement is nigh at hand! The devils who sit as CEOs have wrought their thrones with the alloys of Abaddon! We have warmed ourselves by the hellfires of Hades for too long! Materialism's wicked ways have condemned us all to eternal supplication to the false master Mammon!"[158]

"We don't believe in sin anymore, man," the hairiest hippie said on behalf of the whole group, for he had ironically established himself as the ringleader of the egalitarian conglomerate.

"Yet you think that materialism is evil and returning to Nature is good?" Harold questioned.

"Of course!" the hippie replied. "We have lost our tribal roots! We must return to Nature!"

"Yes," Harold said tiredly, "you have already said that. I assure you that confusion and disagreement does not mean I am hard of hearing. I believe your attempt to become noble savages is born out of a savage fiction.[159] How can one 'return to Nature' having come from Her and being constantly immersed in Her? And what *is* Nature? Are you pretending to dictate to Her what She is?"

"No way, man!" the hippie balked. "Back in the past, we all lived in, like, total harmony with Nature. We planted food and survived from what we planted; we didn't pollute the air and seas with our plastics, and we didn't chisel away at earth's beautiful exterior to suck oil out of her veins for our own personal profit."

"What is this 'back in the past'? Can we judge Nature only by her past forms or also by her potential future productions? What if a quality of Nature is to transform Herself? Are we then ourselves not transformers and creators of new things? Is not technology and artifice then the pinnacle of Nature rather than its ruin? Aren't *you* the one who is actually advocating a refusal of Nature? How can Nature allow for Herself to be divided into what is and is not 'natural'? You've told me only your vision of Nature and now I see what you really mean by returning to It. Only man would be so silly to split himself off from Nature and consider his own creations to be corrupt. If you despise humanity so much, I hope you will lead the charge in bidding farewell to your own body and thus re-establishing in some small quantity that primordial peace that preceded the peopling of this place."

"How can you be so cruel?" the hippie asked with disgust.

"Perhaps it is my nature to be such. Nature is Herself quite cruel. She is harsh, and perhaps I am a bit of a Sadist myself.[160] Nature is unflinching, uncaring; she is constantly building up and breaking down, climbing and catastrophizing, forming and informing and deforming and reforming... beautiful yet useless, bountiful yet wasteful, wonderful yet false."

"I cannot even comprehend what you are rambling about anymore," attackingly exclaimed the second hippie, who ironically preached radical nonviolence.

"I'm not trying to be understood," Harold informed them. "To be understood, one must speak things that are commonplace. Truth is no place for trivialities. I, because I am so generous, leave those for you to be used as weapons in your contradictory causes." Harold walked away and left the hippies with a general hate for him, yet they all later voted for George W. Bush in the election.

Thus huffeth & puffeth Harold to blow the hippie house down.

PART 7:

THE PISTOL OF PRAGMATISM, OR HOW HAROLD EXECUTED TWO TRAITORS TO THEIR OWN TENETS

"Truth is the kind of error without which

a certain being could not live."

–Friedrich Nietzsche

Harold, at this ripe young age of fourteen, considered himself a firm rationalist insofar as he found the mind to be the pinnacle of human evolution and therefore the royal road to Truth. Harold was so rational, in fact, that he uncovered the irrational foundations of rationality. He had found that the root of reason is a form of faith, which is an odious thing to one who is vowed to rationality. Reason assumes that everything is subject to its own law, and reason abides by rules that are not necessarily those of reality. In a conversation with two friends who were perpetually arguing, one being a militant atheist and the other being a staunch Protestant, Harold attempted to illuminate this idea.

"I am most certain that God is not only Creator but is ever-present amongst us, guiding and judging humanity every day since Creation," said Pascal, the staunch Protestant.[161]

"If we accept that God is a being who is omniscient, omnipotent, and omnipresent," argued Immanuel the atheist,[162] "why wouldn't God have arranged the world so as to not even require his guidance and judgment?"

"God created the world and gave humanity free will so that they could have the choice to be sinful or saintly," retorted Pascal, "thereby allowing each of us to prove our own worthiness to abide in the Kingdom of Heaven or the eternal torment of Hell."

"If God is omniscient, doesn't he already know who is going to reside in Heaven and Hell? Aren't the names in the 'Book of Life' already written and predetermined?" Immanuel smiled wryly since thought he had caught Pascal in a bind.

"All is foreseen but free will is given,"[163] Pascal said calmly and without hesitation.

"How is free will free if the decisions to apparent choices are already known ahead of time?"

"It is paradoxes such as these that show the necessity of faith, dear brother," Pascal concluded.

Harold found an opening and interjected, "Reason depends upon language, and language has laws that require certain assumptions to be held for communication to even begin. Consider how sentences are structured: There is a subject who engages in some kind of verb. We already have a syntactical supposition that he world is constructed out of subjects performing various verbs. While this may be intuitively pleasing, it is nonetheless *not* a certain fact. Some would argue that there are unnecessary but useful divisions being made between subjects and their objects or between subjects and their verbs. There is really no consensus on what a 'subject' truly is or how responsible this 'subject' is for its 'verbing.' We have arranged for ourselves a world in which we can live by positing bodies, lines, planes, causes and effects, motion and rest, form and content. Without these articles of faith nobody could now endure life. But that does not prove them. Life is no argument. The conditions of life might include error."[164] Even in his speaking, Harold felt the tremors of terror in approaching such a yawning cavern of uncertainty.

"It has been said that truth is beauty,"[165] Harold continued, 'yet if one is honest then one will soon find some readily available truths that are terrible and ugly. If one strictly adheres to the code of conduct conducive to the highest form of truth-seeking – that is, of a seriousness of intellectual integrity and passion that verges on hardness to the point where one is indifferent to whether truth brings fortune or fatality to oneself – one will necessarily come to edges and abysses that cough and ooze groundlessness. What one does and how one reacts in the face of such uncertainty is the true test of character."

"I'm not sure what you are getting at, my friend," said Immanuel, feeling criticized and attacked for being reasonable.

Harold explained, "I am saying that the rational person criticizing the faithful does not realize the amount of faith in their beliefs."

"You see! I knew Harold was a man of God!" Pascal shouted triumphantly while slapping Harold on the back.

"...and the faithful person criticizing the rational does not realize the amount of reason in their arguments," Harold continued. "Reason and faith are not oil and water; they are really two sides of the same coin of human thought."

"A messy situation, indeed," Immanuel remarked while scratching his head. "What, then, is the resolution to this strange new proposition?"

"How typical of a philosopher to assume that there is a resolution to every problem," Harold said sarcastically. "I believe that a certain solution may be obtained by regarding truth as a matter of breeding."

"I hope this conversation isn't going towards the topic of eugenics," Pascal half-joked.

"In a way, I suppose. One might consider truths not based on their 'truthfulness,' but on the results they breed on those who hold them. We therefore must eliminate truths that breed weakness, and foster the truths that breed strength."

Immanuel asked with honest curiosity, "How is this relevant to our previous discussion?"

"Consider the idea of a God of such qualities as have already been described. To Pascal, this truth is a seed that breeds flowers of happiness, humility, and purpose. To you, this truth is a poison that breeds the tumors of tumult, debasement, and purposelessness."

Pascal exclaimed, "The Parable of the Sower!"[166] while Immanuel simultaneously announced, "The proof of pragmatism!"

"Call it what you may," Harold said, "but I call it compassion."

Pascal noted, "A man of truly saintly disposition!" while Immanuel simultaneously asserted, "A man of truly knowledgeable inclination!"

"Compassion for the flower is cruelty to the weed and compassion for health is cruelty to the poison," Harold continued, "...but who decides what is a 'flower' and what is a 'weed'? Who decides what is a 'poison' and what is a 'curative'? Who decides what is 'strong' and what is 'weak'?"

"God, no doubt!" Pascal said without missing a beat.

Immanuel declared, "A well-established parliament of properly educated peer-review, no doubt!"

"Aye, doubt it not, for each may establish his own rationale suitable to his nature, and if thou art truly joyous that is proof enough of its success." Both Immanuel and Pascal both nodded in approval, for high-flung language exudes undeserved authority.

"I am ashamed of you two!" Harold indignantly ejaculated as both Immanuel and Pascal looked at one another with befuddlement. "I am ashamed and disheartened that you, my mind-girded Immanuel, would be so swayed by such a charismatic and emotional appeal, and that you, my faith-protected Pascal, would be so swayed by such a logical illustration!"

Both friends fell into a mild confusion of self-reflection that Harold used as a time to escape from the Thunderdome of debate, for too much talking always left Harold feeling that he needed to focus on actually saying something.

Thus tieth Harold the ribbon on the present of paradox.

PART 8:

SUPERFICE IS SUPER-NICE, AND OTHER FAILED ATTEMPTS AT CLEVERNESS

"People say sometimes that Beauty is superficial. That may be so.
But at least it is not so superficial as Thought is."
–Oscar Wilde

Harold had entered high school, which he had found had nothing high or noble about it. One day, he was strolling with a female friend, who had been thrown into the jaws of crushing depression after seeing that she had a pimple on her face.

"True beauty is on the inside," she remarked in a thinly-veiled attempt at employing a defense mechanism.

"I actually find organs and entrails to be quite ugly," Harold quipped in return.

"You know what I mean," the girl said in a tone that belied her own mistrust in her statement.

"My lady, I am not sure that I do. First of all, you say 'true beauty,' which I assume you are contrasting against 'false beauty,' perhaps that of appearances. Second of all, you say 'on the inside,' and yet you balked at my taking this to refer to your insides. I suppose you are referring to the content of your character by the phrase 'on the inside,' but tell me: is not the content of our character shown by the quality of our actions? Is not our inside shown by our outside?"

"Yes, I suppose that is true. I just meant I have a beautiful soul, or something," she responded.

"Let's deal with what we have on our plates already before taking another helping of something as indigestible as a 'soul.' Now, I dare say that, really, at the root of your issue, is a belief. Maybe even two beliefs if you are particularly greedy. I personally believe that we can whittle down the world's questions to two in particular: 'What is?' and 'What should be?' We have therefore summarized the basis of metaphysics and ethics, respectively." The girl nodded, even though she had become lost back at the metaphor of plates.

"Now," Harold continued, "we all believe in certain answers to these questions, even though we may not realize it. A quick way to get at them is to ask, firstly, what is True? Secondly, what is Good? Our beliefs about the True and the Good are shortcuts to the house of cards we call our 'understanding of the world.' You must take all of your beliefs, of 'This is true' and 'That is good,' and line them up for inspection."

"I don't know what is true and good, though," the girl meekly retorted, having come back from a daydream just in time to catch the last bit of Harold's lecture.

"What?" Harold gasped in astonishment. "Of course you do! Let me help you start. Your first one is, 'Beauty is on the inside' is True.' Your second one is, 'To not have pimples on your face is Good.' There, you already have given me metaphysical and ethical assertions."

"Where are you going with this, exactly?"

"I am helping you find the root of your existential anxiety, my dear. It's no use to patch up a leak if the pipe is broken. I may be going out on a limb here but not only are your pipes broken, I believe they may have been wrongly fitted to begin with. Now, here is the basic method of transcending the dullness of your rigid belief system. First, take all your beliefs of what is good and true, and the more you believe them, the better. Now, take your statement of belief – let's take the notion that 'Beauty is on the inside is true' – and change the 'true' to 'false' or 'not true.' In this case, you would now have the statement 'Beauty is on the inside is false.' You must plunge into this belief head-first, taking it to be an absolute truth with equal intensity with which you believed the opposite. Really consider how it might be false to say beauty is on the inside."

The girl seemed completely stumped. "Well," Harold helped, "I already gave you one example: your organs do not meet the standard threshold of what is considered beautiful. You might also consider that beauty is an aesthetic quality that requires a tangible object, and your so-called 'soul' or personality does not meet this prerequisite of being beautiful. Roll these ideas around in your mouth until you've gotten a good grasp of their taste. Swallow, rinse, and repeat, preferably without mixing metaphors too badly."

"That sounds like a lot of work," the girl muttered.

"We've only just begun!" Harold exclaimed. "Find your second wind and let us take flight once more. Now, we've already examined the idea that beauty is on the inside is both true and false, so now we have to take the first part of the equation and invert it. We now get the proposition that 'Ugliness is on the inside is true.' Perhaps we might assert that, even as true beauty is internal, true ugliness is as well. I'm sure you can conjure up a few other similar advocates of the Devil if you put yourself to the task. Finally, we come to the fourth proposition: 'Ugliness is on the inside is false.' Glancing around this campus, I can assure that there is plenty of external ugliness. The real test of all of this is to find all four propositions equally true and equally false. We have, with 'X' being your belief, 'X is true,' 'X is false,' 'Not-X is true,' and 'Not-X is false.'[167] The same as what is done with the True must be done with the Good. If we take the opposite of Good..."

"Evil!" the girl declared excitedly. Harold was taken aback, astonished and insulted, and swiftly slapped the girl across the face.

"Never insult my ears again with such silliness! It is a waste of time to perform this practice with principles that are made-up to begin with. No, no, the opposite of Good is not Evil, it is Bad.[168] I do not see why you insist on inserting such falsities into our conversation... 'the soul,' 'evil'... Soon you're going to be telling me about 'free will,' and that would be good for a laugh." The girl emitted a soft whimper as her false sense of agency fell away.

"Where were we? Each of the four propositions of each belief must in themselves be found to be true, false, true and false, as well as neither true nor false... each in their turn. You can quickly see that such a sublime method is the most mystical of all tasks, the destruction of the rule of rationality!"

"So it is 'good' to destroy rationality?" retorted the girl, with a keen and sinister smirk forming on her face.

"Ah, clever girl. I think we can rest assured that, as of now, my brain-bowels are full and we – by the modern standard of decency – we should not fill ourselves any fuller." Harold then gave her a kiss on the cheek and said his goodbyes as he entered the door into his Ethics class.

Thus transcendeth Harold the multiplicity of mind.

PART 9:

A Prod is always Better than A Priori, or how Harold Exposed the Nether-Regions of Philosophy

"But this – is my taste: not good, not bad, but **my** *taste, about which I am no longer secretive or ashamed. 'This – is just my way – where is yours?' Thus I answered those who asked of me 'the way.'*
For **the** *way – does not exist!"*
–Friedrich Nietzsche

Harold meandered into the Ethics class, and his teacher pulled his glasses down to the tip of his nose to say in as professiorial a manner as possible, "Harold. Late again, I see."

"Indeed," Harold replied while stopping to puff up his chest with aristocratic air, "I am late on principle, for I, with Lord Henry, believe punctuality is the thief of time."[169]

"OK, Lord Harold. Take your seat, and you can demonstrate a rebuttal to the first form of ethics which we will treat today. How do we feel about the Golden Rule?"

"I believe I've already made a demonstration of its ridiculousness," Harold said without missing a beat.

"How do you mean exactly?" The professor leaned his body against the lectern in a feigned interest, for his only true interest was seeing himself praised.

"I do not value punctuality. You do. If you were to treat me as you wish to be treated, which appears to be some form of superficial supplication, then I would be left unsatisfied and overappreciated. If I were to treat you the way I wish to be treated, then I would probably be arrested for indecent exposure." The class laughed, even though most did not follow the argument. Harold continued, "If you were to be treated as Lord Alfred Douglas wishes to be treated, you would have trouble walking straight for a week, and we all know you take pride in skillful ambulation."[170]

"Funny..." the teacher mumbled, utilizing the last resort of academics in the face of having no reply: crude sarcasm. "How does Socrates sound to you?"

"I think that 'The unexamined life is not worth living'[171] is simply a chastisement from someone who has spent too much time and energy examining themselves. I think we know from the rudimentary beginnings of psychology that we have today that such a statement can only come from a bit of cognitive dissonance."

"This is a philosophy class, not a psychology class," the teacher said with pride.

"That's where you're wrong, I think." Harold stopped for a

moment to judge whether his teacher's ego had already been wounded enough so that the rest of his ramble would remain unheard. Harold then comforted himself with the notion that he did not need to be heard by his teacher, since his real pleasure came from hearing himself. He continued, "Every philosophy is actually an unconscious autobiography from its author, revealing his or her own prejudices rather than progressing towards knowledge."[172]

Not wanting to set sail on the trepidatious seas of psychology, the teacher deflected, "What is your take on Aristotelian ethics, then?"

"At the risk of misrepresenting the man, I would say that, judging from the size of his beard, he was about half as wise as Socrates and about ¾ as wise as Plato."

"I suppose you are a complete fool, then," the teacher remarked with a sly abuse of power dynamics so common with the disempowered.

"A fool who persists in his folly becomes wise," Harold said in his best impression of an Old English-man.[173] "Really, I think Aristotle's notions were fairly sound, except that he equated virtue – or 'excellence' we should rather say since Christianity has since poisoned the word 'virtue' – with happiness. He believes happiness is virtuous, at least, but a classroom is no place for nuance. Personally, my potential speaks to me saying, 'do not be happy, be great.' And great I was, great I am, and great I shall be; a curse upon daddy super-ego and anyone else who would convince me otherwise!"

"Impressive arrogance, my boy," and the teacher was actually somewhat impressed. "Perhaps you seek pleasure in the manner of hedonistic ethics?"

"I just told you, I do not want to be happy, I do not even want to be pleasured, I want to be great. If I live a life of discontent and tragedy but my name thereby ranks among those of Caesar and Christ, what would petty pleasure plead to make me turn from my melancholic means?"

"Impressive alliteration, this time." The professor asked with a wry smile, "You know it is a hallmark of schizophrenia?"

"There is a fine line between madness and genius, and I prefer to have my feet planted firmly on both sides of any kind of divide. It makes for limber muscles if one stretches in such a way."

"I see, I see," though the teacher did not see at all. "Does anyone else have any agreements or disagreements with hedonism?" No one replied, for everyone else in the class became staunch nihilists at an early age after having woken up from the American dream.

"Alright then. Perhaps you would then demonstrate your view on utilitarianism?" the teacher invited.

Harold started to get up from his seat and the teacher

inquired, "What exactly are you doing?"

"Demonstrating, as you asked." Harold tip-toed up to the front of the class as if to not disturb the deep waking slumber of his colleagues. "If a hedon is a measure of pleasure, and the greatest good is what evokes the most hedons, then what we have is a supremely unethical ethic."

"How do you mean?"

"How I mean is through speech. *What* I mean is this." Harold then swiftly lept over to the professor and pulled down his trousers to his ankles.[174] The class erupted in volcanic laughter as Harold expected. "You see?" Harold said to the teacher while sweeping his arm out across the classroom. "With about 20 students in this class, that action surely produced least 20 hedons. Your humiliation is a mere negative 1 hedon. Even if your humiliation was twenty times the average amout of joy of one of these students, I still would have performed an ethical action."

The red blood of blushing turned quickly to the scarlet of rage, and the teacher sent Harold out of the classroom.

Thus arriveth Harold in the principal's office once again.

PART 10:

NOT TWO AND CERTAINLY NOT THREE OR FOUR, OR HOW HAROLD BECAME AN ADVAITA VEDANTIST

"Understand now that in yourselves is a certain discontent.
Analyse well its nature: at the end is in every case one conclusion.
The ill springs from the belief in two things,
the Self and the Not-Self, and the conflict between them."
—Aleister Crowley

When Harold entered college, he learned that he needed a place to find repose. He found the seriousness of the students absolutely draining: one can only be a pure ocean so long with so many adjoining polluted streams.[175]

After exploring a certain forested area whose emerald inhabitants waved a perpetual greeting to the Pacific Ocean, Harold came upon a rocky outcropping at the edge of a cliff.[176] The multi-colored moss on a rock seemed to bear a striking resemblance to Bob Dylan, so he took it as a divine demand that he listen for any answers in the air.[177] Harold took off his shoes and plopped his bony buttocks on the face of the rock. He entered his pretzel asana and began to meditate upon his mantra of the All-Devourer, "Om Nom Nom."[178]

After an apparent aeon had passed, the mantra seemed to conjure a sexual-electric energy[179] that strangely seemed to emanate from his left pinky finger. Though he was a socialist on the outside, his internal politics were ruled by an iron fascism. Harold therefore increased his attention upon the mantra, not willing to be dethroned as despot of his mind-island. Over and over he repeated the threefold song, but with each repetition, the energy grew stronger, more unignorable, more odious. Soon he could only get so far as the first two of three syllables. Harold threw all his willful weight upon the mantra in an act of Spartan futility.[180] After becoming unable to even remember the first syllable of the mantra, Harold finally said to this strange sense, "Ok, I accept." Harold's world was then plunged into utter blankness.

It was a dreamless sleep; it was a wave-less, reflection-less pond; it was a box that had no boundaries.[181] There was no sense. No space. No thought. No time. No self. Blank, black, absolute nothingness.

...

At some point back within Time, Harold was cast back out of the Abyss[182] like a star falling upon the darkness of the earth.[183] Harold had been spit out of the mouth of Mahavishnu, crawling

Khephra-like[184] out of the Night of Pan,[185] and shot like lightning out of the limitless light into the world once more.[186] He realized that he had been out for a while – not unconscious, but simply not there. He knew a span of time had passed with no idea how long, yet he knew he had not been knocked unconscious. He could not say where he had been or when he had been, so he figured he must have stumbled upon the door to the Nowhere-Nowhen, a place beyond the perceptual parameters of space and time that would be profoundly boring if there were any possibility of there being an identity who could be bored.

It would, in fact, be an error to speak about these things occurring to Harold, for the experience had completely bulldozed the quaint Victorian mansion of his ego. For the sake of simplicity and the abundance of laziness, this most humble narrator will still misleadlingly refer to Harold as the hero and subject of this story. Language should be left to the logicians and excuse-makers, but we have unfortunately not formulated a more adequate means of communication, at least for novels.

"That which uttereth 'I' uttereth falsehood!" the mouth of Harold proclaimed, for it was wont to work with words translated into the Authorized King James version in such times of triumph. Subject and object had not yet differentiated, and Harold had stumbled upon an experiential proof of non-duality. Unfortunately,

Harold had long since disavowed anecdotal evidence as real evidence, so he knew he wouldn't believe his own story. As Harold came back to his Harold-ness and the world came back to its world-ness, he started to move out of his asana. After shifting his weight, he realized he had soiled himself at some point in the denial of duration. "Ah, the anatta enema is certainly the most powerful purgative of all planes,"[187] Harold commented as he waddled penguin-like back down the path from whence he came.

Thus descendeth Harold back into the land of the living.

PART 11:

HAROLD PRACTICES SPIRITUAL OPTOMERY AS A WANDERING PROPHET PREACHING FROM THE POSITIONLESS POSITION[188]

"無問曰、六祖可謂、是事出急家老婆心切。

譬如新荔支剝了殼去了核、送在你口裏、只要你嚥一嚥。"

['The Sixth Patriarch was, so to speak, hurried into helping a man in
an emergency, and he displayed a grandmotherly kindness.
It is as though he peeled a fresh lichi, removed the seed, put it in
your mouth, and asked you to swallow it down.']

–Mumon

After purging himself of the earthly dross, Harold came back from the forest to the people. He passed by a man tuning a stringed instrument, through a straight and narrow way, and then he came upon a tightrope walker.[189] Upon this he achieved momentary *satori*,[190] threw up his hands in the air, and roared, "There are too many lines in this world!" The air was burdened and hungry clouds swagged on the deep.[191]

The crowd that had gathered around the tightrope walker all turned to face Harold. Although most were astonished, the reactions of the crowd varied.[192] About half thought Harold was insane. Some thought he was uttering a metaphysical truth of the illusoriness of the space-marks or lines we place between things, causing us to perceive the Maya of multiplicity[193]... and they all decided on the spot to become his disciples. One old lady spontaneously achieved penetrating insight into the non-arising, primordial ground of all being. One man instantly converted to Christianity for some reason.

Harold saw that he had startled the natives and decided to make an escape. Because of residual delirium from his hibernation sickness,[194] he decided for some reason to awkwardly yell, "No!" before he turned around and dashed in the other direction. Half the crowd took this as confirmation of Harold's insanity. Some took it as a Qabalistic confirmation of his enlightenment, an assertion of his identity with the Ultimate Naught,[195] and so re-dedicated their discipleship with increased fervor. The old lady spontaneously re-entered the world of interdependent co-arising multiplicity. The newly-converted Christian remained a Christian. As Harold scurried away he realized that his time in the forest had slightly atrophied his social skills, so he resolved to refine his rapture and be not so animal.[196]

Harold found a bench to give himself time to think. He was shocked that the obviously evident non-dual nature of Supreme Reality was not intuitively grasped by everyone else. As a man strolled by, Harold jumped up and glared at him. Harold then slapped the man on the back and said, "Is everything alright?" He motioned as if to introduce himself, "I am God, and this farce is my creation."[197] The man was stunned into a mild paralysis. Harold then asked, "Don't you recognize me?" The man's face offered a small furrowing of the brow in reply. Without giving any warning, Harold spun to face the man, held open his eyelid with his fingers, leaned in towards his face, and whispered with determination, "I know I'm in there somewhere..."

At this moment, the disciples caught up to Harold. Seeing this, he scurried away once more. The man's paralysis was then suddenly gone, although he was left with an intense craving for bacon.

Thus cooketh Harold with a Dorje and Phurba.[198]

PART 12:

EVERYTHING IS COMPLETELY ARBITRARY BUT NONETHELESS BEAUTIFUL, AND OTHER WATCHWORDS OF HAROLD'S ATTAINMENT

"Nothingness with twinkles! ...but what twinkles!"
—Aleister Crowley

The disciples quickly caught up to Harold as he had forgotten to eat for the last two days, and one of them grabbed him and pleaded with him, "Please, sir, we know you are a Master of the Temple.[199] You have hidden your identity to the profane but simultaneously revealed it to those who have ears to hear. Anyone who is so good at using blinds must surely be a powerful and wise Adept. Our Temple has lost our connection with the Secret Chiefs.[200] Please become the Hierophant of our Temple! Initiate us into your wisdom with your divine decree from On High!"

This convoluted tirade caused Harold to sober up, recall his formerly civilized manners, and regain his powers of speech. "Fools," he said. They all looked proud, having thought he was identifying them in a symbolic sense with the Qabalistic Zero of The Pure Fool.[201] Harold saw this and shouted, "The *bad* kind of fools!"

They all simultaneously dropped their heads in disappointment. "Haven't you heard?" Harold paused to look for comprehension in the faces of the disciples, but he only saw a bunch of confused cattle. Undaunted, he announced, "There is no initiation!"[202]

After a moment of attempting to process Harold's pronouncement, one disciple shouted, "Restore our Lodge as a true Guru and Initiator!"

Another chimed in, "All the rituals of the old time are black!"

A third pleaded, "Make severe the ordeals!"[203]

"Honestly," Harold confessed, "when it comes right down to it, I'd much rather be a Guru than God, but I don't dare be selfish enough to forgo my duties as Creator of the Universe. You see, *everyone* including myself must make sacrifices, no matter how or where one lives."[204]

The disciples looked singularly puzzled. One disciple soon put into gear his denial defense mechanism and carried on as if he hadn't heard what was just said. He cried, "Bring us the Truth!" Others joined in on the song:

"Bring us Light!"

"And Wisdom!"

"Peace!

"Joy!"

"And Length of days!"

"And Wonder-Tree Sap!"[205]

The barbershop septet of disciples ended their brief petition, and looked upon Harold expectantly.

"None of you seem to understand. I am saying that there is no such thing as initiation. There is none that shall be cast down or lifted up: all is ever as it was!"[206]

The disciples stood in place, completely unphased. Harold tried to explain another way, "Insofar as you are *this*, a mind and body, you are a shadow that will pass and a slave that shall perish. All component phenomena in the world of duality will always be component phenomena in the world of duality, condemned to the cycle of birth into forms, a short though perpetually dynamic life of apparent stability, the dissolution of form, and transformation or rebirth into new forms. Insofar as you are *That*, the boundless Brahman of transcendent reality, you are the united with the sum and source of all existence; the Crowned and Conquering Child would be your name.[207] In Truth, you are That. Always were, are now, and always will be. That Immortal Sun will always be ablaze, whether or not you aware of it, whether or not you do or don't do anything about it. This Self can never die by its very nature of transcending (though somewhat paradoxically also containing) time and space. The normal self and even the normal world of which we are aware will all inevitably pass away by their very nature of being enmeshed in time and space. What can die will never become what doesn't die. Even our consciousness, which by some miracle of Nature is capable of temporarily perceiving and identifying with this Undying Self... even *this* will pass away into nothingness. It is this normal self you fruitlessly hope to be elevated by initiation towards Truth."

The disciples remained unphased, but Harold could tell that he had almost tunnelled all the way through their thick skulls: the prospect of actually being understood seemed possible. He extended yet another explanation, "You think I will bestow some kind of secret knowledge through my words. You think that you will become stronger, wiser, more powerful, and more enlightened by being bestowed degrees. Initiation, in this sense, therefore involves something with a beginning and an end, something that involves becoming more this or less that... a process that involves change, in short. No matter how orderly the chairs are arranged, Elijah's seat will always be empty.[208] The invincible and empty-full non-dual substrate of existence will always be invincible in its empty fulness. The soul is already perfect: perfect purity, perfect calm, perfect silence.[209] Nothing can take away this perfection. Nothing can alter anything about it by its very nature of being beyond all things, by the very perfection of its nature. This is your True Self, and it does not need to be lifted up or cast down; it can't be. The only true initiation would be bringing one's illusory sense of self to the awareness of its own illusoriness, the momentary penetration of the Veil of Mother Matter[210] to see one's original face before one was born, the state of mystic unity where one can state 'I *am* the Truth.'[211] This is said without a hint of pride or conceit; it is said with a supreme confidence to the extent that uttering such a phrase almost seems like a platitude that almost doesn't require being stated since it is so plainly obvious."

The disciples stood in amazement, having finally been phased by Harold's manic diatribe. After a brief moment of silence, several shouts broke out:

"A black brother sent to destroy our holy Order!"[212]

"Choronzon incarnate!"[213]

"I don't think I understood a word of what he said!"

The disciples decided unanimously in favor of abandoning this false prophet, for they preferred the comfort of always agreeing with each other over examining any potentially threatening truths. They stuck their noses up to suck in hot air and continued their search for the Secret Chiefs.

Thus Harold concealeth himself from the profane.

PART 13:

THE RE-ESTABLISHMENT OF THE REALITY OF HALLUCINATION, OR HOW HAROLD BECAME A BUTTERFLY

"A dreamer is one who can only find his way by moonlight, and his punishment is that he sees the dawn before the rest of the world."
–Oscar Wilde

Harold walked down a dark, humid corridor. He felt the walls on both sides – they were close together, almost pressed up against his body. He traveled down this hallway for a while until, finally, he came to a green door. Curiosity combined with a sense of urgency guided his hand to the door handle. He opened the door and a heavy, salty odor washed over him. Harold closed his eyes for a moment in reaction to the smell. When he opened his eyes a moment later, he was met with the sight of an older woman standing inside of the room. Her skin was black – pure, colorless black – which contrasted sharply with her glaringly white eyes that seemed to lack lids. The woman's belly was nearly bursting out from her body – Harold thought he could hear a faint, chaotic drumbeat emanating from it. The woman's face was twisted with emotion – he couldn't tell if it was pain, fear, or anger or all of them at once. The woman's lips were curled back to reveal a set of teeth that would better fit in the the mouth of a lioness. Her triangular tongue flashed across her teeth, licking her lips in anxious desire. The sight of this woman was like a wave of force hitting Harold's eyes.[214] For a brief moment he was stunned, but then he was filled with a terrible, consuming fear. It was a fear so overwhelming that body and mind could do nothing but obey its power. Harold turned and bolted down the hallway in the direction from which he had come. He ran and the walls seemed to be closing in on him. Suddenly, he fell as if the ground disappeared from under him. He plummeted downward leaving behind a blur of flailing limbs and terror. A light began to dawn slowly, then a little quicker... and then a blinding flash. Harold then woke up.

Upon re-entering his material tabernacle of illusion, Harold went next door and recounted this experience to his housemate Pyrrho.[215] When telling this story, Harold failed to mentioned that it was a dream. Once he mentioned waking up, his friend was bewildered and said, "Well there you have it. It was just a dream. It wasn't real."

"Yes, it was a dream," Harold replied, "and it was real."

"Dreams aren't real, Harold. That's why we wake up from them into reality."

"I saw sights," Harold argued while waving his hand in the air as he was wont to do, "I smelled smells, I felt fear. The feelings and sensations were just as strong as those when I'm awake... some of them were even stronger than waking sensations."

"Yes, but that experience ends when you wake up," Pyrrho retorted.

Harold answered without a pause, "And so does waking experience when you sleep."

"Dreams are symbolic, though" Pyrrho rebutted. "The woman is merely the archetype of the terrible Mother, the corridor was perhaps the birth canal. Your fear represents some kind of unconscious, pathological response that you need to work through with a professional, I think."

"And the waking life is somehow different? Don't people clothe themselves in ways that carry symbolic meaning, an outward statement of their inward nature? Don't we perceive people around us in archetypal roles?"

"Yes, but you encountered an archetype in the dream, not a person with a personality."

"Didn't I encounter a particular manifestation of an archetype, just like every woman in bearing a child fulfills the archetypal role of 'Mother'? Just because I didn't stay long enough to learn the lady's name doesn't mean she lacked a personality just like your mother or mine."

"Alright," Pyrrho conceded, "but dreams are subjective worlds. It's only your own and no one else's."

"Is that so? I've heard plenty of accounts of people having the same dream and even interacting with one another therein, and I have the malignant disease of taking people at their word. Anyhow, do we exist in such a non-subjective world when awake? We may be bombarded by the same stimuli as each other, but we all have slightly different senses. Some see better than others. Some can perceive subtle differences in taste that others cannot. Some people are blind or deaf..." Harold closed his eyes, covered his ears, and stumbled around the room for a moment. "Add to this the fact that we all have a unique genetic heritage, a unique upbringing, and a unique cultural context in which we are embedded. When awake, we are all in our own worlds. Our worlds are simply conveniently similar enough to each other that we can agree upon certain things and communicate in a relatively efficient way. Perhaps the real difference is that we've spent so much time and energy discovering, explaining, and mapping the waking world whereas we don't even have so much as a primitive atlas for the dream world."[216] Harold then took in a deep gulp of air as if he had said everything in one breath.

"The dream world violates the laws of reality, though,"

Pyrrho insisted.

"You mean they violate the laws of physics of the waking world."

"Same thing."

"Is it, my boy? That simply belies your own prejudice that 'waking is real' and 'dream is illusion.' Some Eastern philosophers would argue that they are both illusions, and I hear from reputable authorities that they are usually quite wise. Perhaps we are more realistic in dreams because we more readily acknowledge they're illusions. I prefer to see it inversely: waking and dream experiences are both real, though the two worlds may function through different or even contradictory laws."

"This all reminds me of Chuang Tzu who couldn't figure out whether he was Chuang Tzu dreaming he was a butterfly or if he was a butterfly dreaming he was Chuang Tzu."[217]

"Indeed! That is exactly what I'm talking about! Some people prefer to be Chuang Tzu and some prefer to be the butterfly. Some people try to escape from the terror of the waking world by falling asleep and some people try to escape from the terror of the dreaming world by waking up. I don't particularly see any reason to presume one is more realistic than the other."

"I suppose this dialogue will end with one of us waking up and realizing this is all a dream?" Pyrrho said snidely.

"No, that would be far too cliché."

Thus wandereth Harold in the world of the wide-awake.[218]

PART 14:

HAROLD WEAVES, AND IS CLOTHED WITH DERISION; MEDITATES, AND IS PLAGUED BY ASTRAL VISION[219]

"We may consider all beings as parts of ourselves,
but it is more convenient to regard them as independent.
Maximum Convenience is our can[n]on of 'Truth.'"
–Aleister Crowley

Having become bored with Malkuthian mummery, Harold determined to discover the conventions of the more subtle planes.[220] He entered a diner and asked for a glass of water.

While the waitress was away, Harold arranged his temple for his travels. He placed a napkin on his lap as his lambskin apron, arranged the dinner plate as his disk, stood the salt and pepper shakers as Solomonic pillars, the butter knife became his dagger, and his fork became his three-pronged wand of the Holy Fire. The waitress came back with his cup of water, which he solemnly set on his plate as his holy chalice.[221] Although he could not quite remember the correct procedures, Harold drew deep, deep his breath, slowly brought his forefinger to his lips, and threw it outwards while yelling, "Apple pancake diamond hoes!"[222] A Jesuit priest sitting near Harold was instantly cast into the Qliphoth from whence he came.[223]

In his mind's eye, Harold imagined an automatic door in front of him. He gave the Sign of the Enterer upon which the doors opened,[224] he floated weightlessly through the astral portal,[225] and darkness was upon the face of the deep. The world was without form and void[226] until Harold figured himself as a Blue Angel[227]; he shot upwards, propelled by the power of pre-regulation, destroyer-class, solid-fuel recoil boosters.[228] After expending his energy, Harold ended up in the sixth deva-world of Tusita.[229] There he encountered a luminescent Bodhisattva perched upon a throne of lotus flowers.

The androgynous ascended one announced, "I am Tathagatagarbha Madhyamaka Avalokitesvara Padmasambhava Prajnaparamita Nirodha-Samapatti!"[230]

"Harold, nice to meet you."

"What brings you into this realm, mortal?"

"I was just on my way to the City of the Pyramids, and I must have gotten lost."[231]

"With what selfish aim have you draw your arrow of aspiration?"[232] the Bodhisattva assumingly inquired.

"I heard the barkeep Babalon ferments the very best wine, and I figured I would give it a try."[233]

"Young one," the Bodhisattva said with exaggerated compassion, "you have yet to even enter the stream. You have at least twenty more reincarnations before you may become a once-returner."[234]

"Just because you cannot understand one who speaks in riddles does not mean the riddler is fettered," Harold replied.[235]

"The spoke of Right Speech is broken on your wheel of Eightfold renunciation," the Bodhisattva commented.

"And Typhon, Hermanubis, and the Sphinx all struggle in a constant battle to up-end one another on my rim, but I abide unmoved in the center thereof."[236]

"One who has such conceit can never achieve a favorable rebirth in the pure abodes!"

"What, then, got you to this lovely, formless place, might I ask?"

"I have taken the most austere vow[237] out of my boundless compassion for suffering to return endlessly into the realm of Samsara until the even the basest stone has achieved Buddhahood."

"I pray that you remind me of the Three Characteristics of all that resides in the realm of Samsara," Harold asked as a leading question, for he figured himself as being part-lawyer and part-psychologist.

The Bodhisattva replied, "All is impermanent. All is

unsatisfactory. All is without substantial self."

"Who, then, are you seeking to save? And who is doing the saving? Knowledge is the curse of the seeing, and ignorance the blessing of the blind. It is not the mineral inhabitants of earth that require Buddhahood; only a god would be so vain as to think that the perfection of simplicity of stones somehow require the convoluted compassion-cries of a redeemer. Both Nirvana and Samsara are Perfect. The Perfect doesn't require any further fixing; the only thing to do in this case is experience the play of Perfection with the natural attitudes of gratitude and enjoyment."

Thereupon was the Bodhisattva disabused of his martyr-complex: he was liberated from his vow of liberation, the heavens were transfigured, and a cherubic chorus rang out, sending lotus-songs of liberation to the six quarters.

Thus transcendeth Harold the sixth deva-world.

PART 15:

The Destructive Deity's Didactic Delusions, or how Ra-Hoor-Khuit Tripped on his Double-Wand of Power[238]

"Balance against each thought its exact opposite!
For the Marriage of these is the Annihilation of Illusion."
–Aleister Crowley

Harold proceeded upward in the supra-mundane planes; at least it appeared to be upward. When one has no law of gravity nor earthly frame of reference, all directions are equally every other. Upon traveling in his body of light for an astral aeon or two, Harold arrived at a temple with Ancient Egyptian decor. Seeing as how Harold was wont to imagine himself as having been a high priest of Amon-Ra in the 11th Dynasty,[239] he decided to explore.

Upon arriving at the top of some sandstone steps, Harold was confronted by a hawk-headed god[240] who barred him from proceeding further.

The god shrieked from his curved beak, *"En aat am-a shu-t em neter!"*[241]

"Gesundheit," Harold said in reply. "Do you happen to speak

the Holy Language?"[242]

"Who art thou that dost fly to my firmamental fane?"[243] the god questioned.

"I am the Stealer of Sorrows! I am the Breaker of Winds! I am He that ever Goeth, being in myself quite Restless! Most people call me Harold, though."

"Hail, Harold."

"I am Hale Harold, indeed; free of all infirmity.[244] And who might you be?"

"Ra-Horakhty, Immortal Sun of the Two Horizons."

"I thought you were named Ra-Hoor-Khuit?"

"You can blame that blunder on Budge; he was not a very good listener."[245]

"Perhaps you might take responsibility for always being so unclear?"

"I am the clear light itself. My very being bursts with the flaming sword of superconsciousness. Do what thou wilt shall be the whole of the Law."

"A very brief law, indeed. How is one to do one's Will?"

"Even as all stars soar through the night-sky, all beings abide in the way of the Universal Will. Seek that, and then do it!"

"Referring to a Universal Will is as useless for finding one's own individual Will as referring to the idea 'Art' is in deciding to create a painting," Harold argued, "or referring to the idea 'Music' in deciding to create a song. Perhaps you might further elucidate the nature of this Will that I may find it?"

"Will is a flame,"[246] Ra-Horakhty replied, "hidden in the core of the being of all that lives."

"Are not Autumn and Winter as necessary as Spring and Summer?" Harold gibed.

"Will is pure,[247] unadulterated and undiluted," Ra-Horakhty riposted.

"Isn't it the impurities in rocks that give them their colorful luster?"

"Will is ever-joyous, bliss-infused and *ananda*-adorned!"

"Evolution stagnates without catastrophe," Harold retorted. "You should know that, O Baby-sitter of the Blasted Tower.[248] Besides, is not suffering the great deliverer from the dross of dead desires?"

"Will is one-pointed, for a nail with many heads cannot perform its purpose of penetration."[249]

"Is not the peak of a mountain supported by a substructure in all directions? Is not the apex of a pyramid uplifted by virtue of its four-fold foundation?"

"Will is divine, aloof and alone in the Supernal sanctuary."[250]

"Do not trees grow tall to have their leaves lap up sunlight by their roots cracking demonic rocks and sucking up the black, chthonic waters of the underworld?"

"Do you want my help or not?" Ra-Horakhty scoffed.

"Merely having curiosity does not imply that I require help of any sort. Do you want *my* help?"

Ra-Horakhty crushed an universe in frustration, and threw his Ankh to the ground with a grumble.[251] His hands having been occupied until then, he suddenly had room to hold the Stone of the Philosophers. The god thereby automatically accomplished the Great Work, for the initiator is nothing but a skillful frustrator and Harold was a dextrous disheartener.

Thus turneth Harold the tables from covenant to combat.

PART 16:

TERMA TUPPERWARE, OR HOW INTUITION GUIDED HAROLD ASTRAY

"Experience teaches us no less clearly than reason,
that men believe themselves to be free, simply because
they are conscious of their actions and unconscious of the
causes whereby those actions are determined."
–Baruch Spinoza

After passing beyond the realm of Ra-Horakhty, Harold found himself in a strange landscape littered with Greco-Roman ruins. Harold ran his palm along a fallen pillar, wondering what hidden hand of his unconscious had guided him to this plane. He glanced up and saw a sign that read, "Wisdom" with an arrow pointing up.

Harold considered that it could be a statement about how what men call wisdom is really just a bunch of hot air; or perhaps it was a vestige of an Abrahamic prophet who claimed that true wisdom comes from "above"; or maybe the arrow was actually not an arrow at all but a point of light that burst into three protruding lines to represent the illumination of wisdom. Harold decided to take it as a road sign and started to walk forward in search of this wisdom.

After a few minutes, Harold came upon a shovel stuck in the ground. He picked it up and got a sudden intuition to go dig under a cluster of weeds. Harold jammed the shovel into the dry, crusted earth and feverishly flung the dust in all directions. He hit something hard and started clawing at the object.

Harold had once heard that certain Tibetan adepts had buried certain treasures of illuminated wisdom for someone who was destined to find and reveal it to humanity at some unknown future date. He figured that it would make sense for these *termas* to be hidden on the astral plane, only retrievable by those with the spiritual fitness to traverse these subtle backlands of the soul. Harold saw that the object was a small, black, carved box, which he picked up and, with extreme excitement, flipped open the lid in hopes of finding the next *Tao Teh Ching, Bhagavad Gita, Heart Sutra,* or *Principia Discordia.*

Once open, there was nothing inside the box except a small slip of paper with nothing written on it. Harold picked it up and turned it over to see if there was anything on the other side. All he found was a crude drawing of genitalia, not unlike those found in many bathroom stalls. "For how impermanent everything is," Harold thought to himself, "some things are remarkable in never changing."

He pondered whether the note may be a remnant of some phallic cult who worshipped the generative power of the universe manifested in the human procreation. Perhaps it was, in fact, what the sign and his silly inuition were directing him to, and the paper inside the container represented the hidden creative Wisdom of Chokmah inside the black box of Binah.[252] Maybe it was a crude attempt at humor to show the cruel nature of the universe being a joke of the General at the expense of the Particular.[253] Harold then heard shouting in the distance and decided to go check it out. He manifested an astral pen and drew a vagina on the other side, muttering something about gender equality.

Thus yonieth Harold the lingam.

PART 17:

GLUTTONY AND PRIDE, OR THE FAILINGS OF MAGICIANS AND MYSTICS

"Simplicity is the ultimate sophistication."
–Leonardo Da Vinci

After following the sound of shouting, Harold came upon two people at the entrance of another Temple, for the astral plane has an abundance of shrines and synagogues as the rent is quite low. One of the people was a woman, dressed in an azure kimono, while the other was a man, dressed in scarlet armor.[254] Harold came upon their discussion and listened intently.

"The path of mysticism is the only pure way," the woman insisted, "for the work of magick always fall prey to the Qliphotic desires of material pleasure."

"A true magician works only to accomplish his Will," argued the man. "Whether or not this involves material pleasures is a moot question. The path of magick is well-founded, for it does not neglect worldly necessities."

"If one stares too long into the Abyss, it may stare back at you,"[255] the woman retorted, "and to dally in the land of attachment is to condemn oneself to inevitable sorrow. The path of mysticism guards against the falsity of interpretation, for the mystic goal is beyond all words and all images."

"The magician may create and destroy illusions if he so Will, and besides, who has tread the Path of the Wise without a signpost or symbol? It is the path of magick that will guide men aright, for the mystic ecstasy leaves one in a crude and childish condition, emaciated and unfit to communicate truth to the world."

"Before and after satori one may chop wood and carry water," the woman rebutted. "It is not a necessary prerequisite to attainment that one is cloistered and unhealthy. The mystic path is the straight and narrow that does not concern itself with unnecessaries."[256]

The man replied, "The Middle Pillar is supported by balanced columns on both sides, for the wand of the Will is buttressed by balanced mercy and severity.[257] A magician is built as a pyramid with a strong base, the mystic resolves to reach heaven like a jet with engines but no wings for steadying."

Harold thought to interject but thought to himself, "It is only the intellectually lost that ever argue,"[258] and he continued on past them into the Temple.

Thus passeth Harold through the pylons of false dilemmas.

PART 18:

DISSOLVE AND COAGULATE, OR HOW HAROLD AVOIDED PAYING HIS KARMIC DEBT

"[666] therefore said: Let me declare this Work under this title: 'The obtaining of the Knowledge and Conversation of the Holy Guardian Angel,' because the theory implied in these words is so patently absurd that only simpletons would waste much time in analysing it. It would be accepted as a convention, and no one would incur the grave danger of building a philosophical system upon it."[259]

–Aleister Crowley

After passing into the Temple, Harold was met with a long hall with several veils draped across the room. After pushing his way through them he came to a final diaphonous sheet that cloaked a throne from his view.

"Greeting of Earth and Heaven,[260] O abrasive one," a soothing voice called from the hidden throne as a bell tolled from above.

"Who rang that bell?" Harold asked in a shrill voice.[261]

"Twas I, child, for the time for our meeting has come. I am your Holy Guardian Angel." The diaphonous sheet dissolved and left Harold face to face with a young woman with jet black skin.

"I am not convinced," Harold stubbornly declared. "My knowledge of symbology leads me to believe that white is the color of holiness and black of ignorance."

The Angel responded, "That which radiates light may be white, indeed, but only a broken vessel would allow such a leak. That which absorbs all light is black to the eye."

"Fine, fine, so mote it be. You know... I've come a long ways and always endured travails by my own wit and wisdom. Where were you in all those times of trouble if you are my Guardian?"

"My hand is invisible though its guidance is constant. I am a Guardian, certainly, but I guard the truth. Truth cannot be approached except through endless trials and tribulations."

"If you are an angel, a minister of God, I'd like to ask to speak to your manager since those in the lower hierarchies never seem to know anything at all."

"I can only be a messenger and envoy from On High, for the ultimate union is beyond all form, force, color, name, and distinction. As long as you are still here, so must I be, but when you give your last drops of selfhood we'll both be free."

"Is there a blood bank around here where I can make the donation?"

"Yes, it is over there, in the City of the Pyramids." The Holy

Guardian Angel pointed at a neon sign that said as much.

"Ah, how could I have missed it! You've been helpful after all – thank you!" Harold started to trot off.

"Remember – before consummation, you are required to give all you have! And..." The Angel's voice faded off as Harold suddenly came to in the realm of Malkuth.

"...after you consume your meal, you are required to pay, sir." The waitress stood unamused as she had been standing beside Harold for the last few minutes repeating herself as he sat, eyes closed, grasping his fork and mumbling incoherently.

"I apologize," Harold said while suddenly standing up, "but I have to inform you that the individual who walked in here and ate a meal is not the same person as the one who you speak to now."

"Ah, the old mystic's excuse for not paying their bills. Like I've never heard that one before. If you don't have any money, get the hell out and don't come back."

Harold left the building, thanking the gods that they don't employ the IRS to track karmic debt. He was slightly amused, slightly disappointed, happy yet not completely satisfied. He did not walk into a sunset nor did he live happily ever after. He simply kept doing his thing, and he eventually died in obscurity in a non-comical way. That's life.

Thus endeth Harold the tiresome interlude.

[151]

PART II:
THELEMA
MADHYAMA-PRATIPAD

CHAPTER 1:
INTRODUCTION TO THELEMA
MADHYAMA-PRATIPAD

"Madhyama-Pratipad" means "Middle Way" or "Middle Path." This refers to the Path expounded by the Buddha. Thelema is also a Middle Way insofar as "Equilibrium is the basis of the Work,"[262] and our method of love under will involves the passionate union and transcendence of opposites.

Our Middle Way is based on Equilibrium just like in Buddhism, but – unlike the typical explanation of the Middle Path – we do not avoid extremes to come to rest in moderation. On the contrary, we are to "exceed! exceed!" and "Strive ever to more!"[263] Rather than avoiding the extremes of asceticism and hedonism to rest in the average or mean thereof, we seek to experience the extreme of both asceticism and hedonism. We thereby naturally come to an equilibrium that is fuller, more aware, more experienced, and more capable of adapting to the varying circumstances of life. It is like the difference between the equilibrium of a thin stem protruding from the ground and the equilibrium of a pyramid with its base extended firmly in the four directions. In this way, many of the basic truths of Buddhism are not neglected within Thelema but they are re-interpreted, re-examined, transmuted, or even stood on their heads. The truth of the impermanence of all things can be seen in *Liber AL vel Legis* when it is said that things "pass & are done," yet the First Noble Truth of Buddhism is flipped around when it is also proclaimed in the same line that "Existence is pure joy."[264] The examples are endless, and I hope that the chapters of this section will help illuminate some of these connections.

The Buddhist sutras (or "suttas" in Pali) are incredibly vast in their scope, both in terms of their content as well as in their style. The Theravada suttas are incredibly different from those of Mahayana, which are also incredibly different from those of Vajrayana. Even within these different "schools," there are vast differences as, for example, the difference between the more Hindu-influenced Mahayana suttas of India, the "Pure Land" Mahayana suttas, and the more Taoist-influenced Mahayana suttas of China and Japan. Some, like the *Dhammapada,* are very straightforward and practical while others, like the various texts of Zen, are often intentionally obscure and difficult. Nonetheless, I have attempted to retain and portray the spirit of these varying Buddhist approaches in this Thelema Madhyama-Pratipad.

CHAPTER 2:
THE SHADOW SERMON[265]

"Remember all ye that existence is pure joy; that all the

sorrows are but as shadows; they pass & are done;

but there is that which remains.

–Liber AL vel Legis

Thus I heard from someone once:[266]

On one occasion a Master, called the Venerable None,[267] was staying at a Lodge with one thousand disciples. There, the Venerable None addressed the disciples:

"Disciples, All is but as a shadow.

What is this 'All' that is shadow?

The eyes are shadows, shapes are shadows, consciousness arising from the conjunction of eye with shapes are shadows, also whatever things are felt as pleasurable, painful, or neither-pleasure-nor-pain that arise from this eye-consciousness are also shadows. Shadows of what?

Shadows of the darkness of sorrow, of the darkness of ignorance, of the darkness of illusion.[268] All the shadows are dark with birth, life, and death,[269] dark with sorrow, with pain and regret, with failure and fear.[270]

Not just the eye, but the ears are shadows, and the sounds are shadows. The nose is a shadow, and smells are shadows. The tongue is a shadow, and tastes are shadows. The body is a shadow, and all bodily sensations are shadows. Even the mind is a shadow, and all thoughts are shadows. Consciousness itself is a shadow, created by the contact of the eye, ear, nose, tongue, body, and mind with shapes, sounds, smells, tastes, bodily sensations, and thoughts. Anything that arises dependent on this consciousness, whether experienced as pleasure, pain, or neither-pleasure-nor-pain, are all shadows. Shadows of what? Shadows of the darkness of sorrow, of the darkness of ignorance, of the darkness of illusion. All the shadows are dark with birth, life, and death, dark with sorrow, with pain and regret, with failure and fear. The shadows of All are like an unreal city, an illusion appearing under the brown fog of a winter noon.[271]

The shadows of the world are enchanting. They draw us into their sorrow, their pain and regret, their failure and fear.

Seeing the shadows as enchanting illusions, the noble disciples of the Master disentangle themselves from the illusion, from the darkness of the shadows. The noble disciple, hearing this truth and seeing through the illusory enchantment of all shadows, disentangles herself from the enchantment. The noble disciple therefore becomes disenchanted with the eye, disenchanted with shapes, disenchanted with the eye-consciousness that arises from eyes and shapes interacting, and disenchanted with any pleasure, pain, or neither-pleasure-nor-pain that arises therefrom.

Likewise, the noble disciple becomes disenchanted with the ear, the nose, the tongue, the body, and the mind. The noble disciple becomes disenchanted with sounds, smells, tastes, bodily sensations, and thoughts. The noble disciple becomes disenchanted with ear-consciousness, nose-consciousness, tongue-consciousness, body-consciousness, and mind-consciousness.

When the noble disciple truly attains this disenchantment, the darkness fades away. With the fading of the darkness, the noble disciple attains enlightenment. When enlightened, there arises Understanding.[272] The Understanding speaks thus: 'Birth, life, and death are all enchantments of shadow. The

[158]

holy life of a disciple is done, and there is Nothing beyond these shadows.'"273

That is what the Venerable None said. The disciples were joyous, and the hearts of all thousand disciples were enlightened, piercing the darkness of the shadows so that they were enchanted and entangled no more.

CHAPTER 3:
THE DIAMOND TEACHING[274]

"There is a solemnity of the silence.

There is no more voice at all.

So shall it be unto the end."

–Liber Liberi vel Lapidus Lazuli

Thus I heard from someone once:

V.V.V.V.V., the Light of the World, once ventured into a bar called the City of the Pyramids, and She ordered a drink.[275]

Seven disciples saw the Master and approached Her. The Light greeted Her disciples as she is wont to do: She smiled at them and then kissed each of their feet. The Awakened None[276] then rose to stand erect and said:

"Do what thou wilt shall be the whole of the Law."

The disciples replied in harmony:

"Love is the law, love under will."[277]

The first disciple approached V.V.V.V.V. and asked of Her:

"Venerable Master, how do I find my Will?"

The Light of the World beamed a smile, sat down on Her barstool, and said:

> "Child of Earth, dearest Brother, this Will is not yours. You do not possess a Will.
>
> You do not possess a Will like you possess your clothes, your television, or your car. You do not possess your Will like you possess a job, money, or titles of secular or occult distinguishment. You do not possess your Will like you possess thoughts, beliefs, hopes, fears, desires, or expectations. No, you do not possess a Will at all. If anything, Child, the Will possesses you.
>
> If you possess something, it is able to be possessed. It can be grasped with the hands, or it can be grasped with the mind. If you can grasp something with your hands, there is always a way to put it down and grasp something else. If you can grasp something with your mind, there is always a way to forget it and grasp something else. The Will can never be completely put down; the Will can never be completely forgotten.
>
> If something can be grasped, it can be encompassed by something greater. A physical object can be encompassed by

the hands, and it is therefore able to be grasped. A mental object can be encompassed by the mind, and it is therefore able to be grasped. The Will can not be grasped, it cannot be possessed because you are not greater than the Will. The Will is greater than you. The Will not something inside of you, you are something inside of the Will. The Will is not something controlled and moved by you, you are controlled and moved by the Will.

My Brother, you do not contain a Will; the Will contains you. Therefore, though it may be practical in regular speech, to say 'my True Will' is an error.

Child of Earth, you do not possess a Will so therefore you do not find a Will as something you would find and then possess. You do not find the Will, the Will finds you. It is not the Will that is hiding itself, it is you who hides from the Will.

What makes you believe that the Will is something that needs finding, my Brother? Is it lost? Did someone take it from you? Did you accidentally throw away your Will with your trash? In your search, did you put up posters offering a reward for its safe return, no questions asked?[278]

If you search for something, you have some idea as to what it is you are looking for. The Will, thankfully, does not conform to your ignorant notions of what it is or what it should be. The Will is. And this 'is' is constantly becoming. Even if you were to find and catch the Will like an escaped animal, when you turned to announce your having pinned it down, it will already be gone.

If you seek to find something, you admit it is not with you. The Will is already with you. It *is* you, more You than you. Your searching for Will is like someone searching maddeningly for their wedding ring while it is on their finger the entire time. The Will is on your finger already, Brother. Therefore: Rejoice!"

The first disciple smiled, bowed, and silently clinked his glass against the Light of the World's.

A second disciple approached the Master, bowed her head, and asked:

"Most Wise Initiatrix: How do I know my Will?"[279]

The Light of the World smiled once more and replied:

"Little Sister in the Light, your intentions are noble, yet I fear they are misguided.

[163]

To know a thing is not to acquire a thing. A thought of the Will is not the Will.

Should you obtain all the thorough and intricate knowledge of the nature of a gold coin – knowing its weight, its size, its inscription, its place of minting, its purpose for distribution, its past, current, and future owners – you would still be no richer.

Even so, should you come to know the thorough and intricate knowledge of your True Will, you would be no more an Adept than before acquiring that knowledge.

Nonetheless, just as knowledge of a gold coin will help you to distinguish its impostors – a copper coin, a silver coin, or a coin of fool's good – even so will knowledge of the Will aid in distinguishing its impostors.

True Will is not a thing known. Like sand, it will slip through your fingers upon grasping it. Like a shadow in the corner of your eye, it will disappear once you turn to closely examine it.

True Will is not a thing known. It is enacted; it is accomplished, and yet it is never fully acted, never fully accomplished.

It is better to act rashly than to stagnate in pondering and, little Sister, your question is rash indeed. You are therefore well on your way! Therefore: Rejoice!"

The disciple bowed once more, raised her glass, and said "To Nuit!" The Master responded likewise and turned her attention to the third disciple who approached slowly and confusedly:

"Venerable None, I ask of you: Who is a Master of the Temple? How can we recognize him?"

The Light of the World furrowed her brow in faux concentration and stated:

"Who indeed is such an Adept? His Being is such that it calls up questions rather than answers.

If a man were to say, 'I am a Master of the Temple,' you can hastily dismiss such an impostor. The Master of the Temple is one who has drained out every drop of self, every drop of personality, every drop of identity, every drop of separateness into the Cup of Universal Life and Impersonal Emptiness. Therefore, he that utters 'I' declares in such a sentence a lack of such an attainment. Even one who thinks 'I' declares himself unready to take such a leap into the Abyss. Yet, even so, a God has a tendency to veil Itself in illusion, so even this is no sure test!

See that train off in the distance? Mighty and terrible is its motion, penetrating space with one-pointed precision and determination. It is an image of the True Will in this way. Inside each of us, an organ exists that cannot be excised; it is like a thread in our Veil of Incarnation that cannot be pulled out without unraveling the entire tapestry. This organ is the ego-making faculty, called *ahamkara* by the Brahmins. It is like the creaking of gears in a machine, constantly whining and insisting with each turn, 'I,' 'I,' 'I'...

That train in the distance: see its puffs of smoke? With every lurch forward it puffs up smoke, and each puff insists, 'I,' 'I,' 'I'... Though it may pollute the air, though it has virtually no effect on the train running its course, it puffs and puffs. Such is the way our body works – such is the unnecessary necessity of incarnating into this world of multiplicity. The average man does not know this is the case and mistakes the smoke as being essential. The Master of the Temple simply knows it for what it is: a puff of smoke, forming, appearing to have a solid shape for a moment, and then dispersing, again and again.

The Master of the Temple sleeps, rises, works, rests, speaks, eats, shits, breathes, and farts just like the rest of us. The Master of the Temple feels pain and pleasure, thinks pro and con, moves to and fro, just like the rest of us. There is no difference from an ignorant fool and a Master of the Temple in this way.

Yet, the Master of the Temple works unassuaged of purpose, for every moment is whole in itself, a purpose sufficient unto itself, there being no one therein to strive for 'better' or 'more.'

The Master of the Temple works delivered from the lust of result, for he tends the garden of life that he may tend the garden, caring neither if there are fruits or no.

The Master of the Temple is like a spinning wheel: the center of this wheel is hollow, and the water droplets of experience cannot cling to the rim.

And might I ask why one would want to recognize a Master of the Temple? Should you use this knowledge to look up his address, knock on his door, and pester him? Do you think he can do or say something to magically bestow your Will upon you as if it were a gift to receive? Do you approach him as if he has authority in some matters to settle one of your petty disputes?

Little brother, there is one goal that we all have, one duty, and only one right and nothing else: Do what thou wilt. Trouble not your spirit to recognize a Master of the Temple, nor an Exempt Adept, an Adeptus Major, nor an Adeptus Minor, nor a Practicus, nor a Philosophus, nor a Zelator, nor a Neophyte, nor a Probationer. Care not to identify or categorize others at all – just as you have a sole right to do your Will, so do they, regardless of their grade.

Do not trouble them, and do not let them trouble you: tend the garden and nothing else; tend it for the sake of tending it, for there is joy in this work whether it brings fruit or no. There is no true work other than this work; there is no true joy other than this joy. It is a difficult task; it is the most difficult because it is the simplest possible task of all. Therefore: Tend thou thine garden... and Rejoice!"

The fourth disciple stepped forward and anxiously inquired:

"Venerable None, what are the best ritual implements to procure for my Temple? What are the best books to acquire for my knowledge?"

The Light of the World laughed as if she was playing her favorite game. She took a sip of her drink, cleared her throat, and asked:

"My beloved Brother in the Light, are there not millions of grains of sand on a riverbank?"

The disciple thought for a moment and replied:

"Yes, Venerable None, there are millions of grains of sand on a riverbank."

The Light of the World continued:

"Brother, if there were a million rivers in each world, each with a million grains of sand, would there not be many grains of sand?"

The disciple replied:

"Yes, Venerable None, there would be millions of millions of grains of sand."

The Master continued.

"If there were a million grains of sand in each river, and there were a million rivers in each world, and there were many worlds around each star, and there were millions of stars in the sky, would there not be many grains of sand?"

The disciple replied immediately:

"Beloved Master, there would be an inconceivably vast amount of grains of sand."

The Master nodded and said:

"If half of all these grains of sand contained the most expensive and lavish ritual implements and other items of luxury that you could own, and the other half of all these grains of sand contained the most comprehensive and rarified bits of knowledge you could possess, would you not be incomprehensibly rich and knowledgeable?"

The disciple became slightly intoxicated at the mere thought:

"Venerable None, there would be no one who had ever come close to having even a millionth of a millionth of my richness and my knowledge."

The Master nodded again and said slowly:

"Yes, my Brother, that is true. Yet, if you had a single droplet of Will you would be incomparably richer and more knowledgeable than this. You appear to me to have far more than a single droplet and space for many more. Therefore: Rejoice."

A fifth disciple impatiently announced his question at the last word of the Master:

"What can one do to be one who Wills?"

The Light of the World answered as quickly as the question was asked:

"Aye, my Brother: do. That is indeed a key to the secret vault of gnosis.

Striving after the Will is to stray from the Will. All the many plans and purposes and wishes and whims that you have are so many dust motes upon the face of the clear mirror of Will. Whosoever stops striving, stops doing, they will come that much more into the pure Will. Thus it is said that not-doing is true doing. Whosoever is unassuaged of purpose comes that much more into the pure Will. Thus it is said that purposelessness is true purpose. Whosoever is delivered from the lust of result will come that much more into the pure Will. Thus it is said that no results is true success.

Even so, one who is newly planted in the soil of the Great Work, an initiate beginning on the Path, one does not simply refrain from doing, refrain from setting purposes, or refrain from seeking certain results. A Master knows her True Self, and therefore meditation in order to achieve this awareness is absurd. A new initiate does not know his True Self, though it is always present, so meditation is prescribed to induce this awareness. This is therefore why many disciplines are prescribed for the new initiate. This is why virtues and vices are explained to the new initiate. This is why one goal is better than another goal for the new initiate.

The folly of this is to take it for truth rather than expendiency. The folly of this is to become rigid and stagnant in these expediencies. This is therefore why many Masters speak from the perspective of the goal attained, explaining that the Will was with you from the beginning. From this perspective, we speak of truth rather than expendiency.

All the many things we do are so many deviations from the Path. It is as if you left your home in search of your home. Even so, all of these deviations are still Will. All of these doings are still Will. All of these purposes are still Will.

All we do is what the Will moves us to do. All we have done is what the Will has moved us to do. All that we can and will do is what the Will moves us to do. Wherefore would a man seek what cannot fail to be accomplished?

Yet there is a strange mystery of this Will that it can give the appearance of divorcing itself from itself. Even so, this is no cause for sorrow; on the contrary, it is that which makes possible the chance of union. Leaving our home in search of our home makes coming back all the more joyful. Therefore: Rejoice!

A sixth disciple approached, bowed, and asked:

"Venerable Master, why did you buy a drink?"

The Master smiled and said:

"When the body becomes thirsty, what do you do?"

The disciple replied:

"One procures a glass and fills it with a drink."

The Master smiled again and continued:

"And when you are finished, what do you do?"

The disciple replied:

"One cleans the glass."

The Master replied:

"Exactly."

The disciple looked puzzled, and upon seeing this, the Master continued:

> "This is your answer, but I can see it is not satisfying to you. I am not yet finished with my drink, and I will discuss this further.
>
> The question you are asking is, 'Why does a Master do what she does?' The answer is, of course, that there is no 'why' in the conventional sense. The Masters acts such because the Master could not have acted otherwise. It is, so to speak, a pure expression of the True Nature of the Master. If a Master speaks, it is an expression of this True Nature. If a Master farts, you have received the sermon for the day. Every action of a Master is a microcosm of her attainment, even the most subtle or obscure.
>
> To ask a Master why she has or has not done something is equivalent to asking why a flower blooms and wilts, why a river runs its course, why the moon waxes and wanes, why the dog barks, and why the bird sings. If this seems absurd, why is it less absurd to ask this of a Master? Why is it less absurd to ask this of anyone?

The question 'Why' is only satisfied with 'reasons.' The answer is expected in the form of, 'I did this because of that' or 'I did that because of this.' Usually, we speak on the level of expendiency, and identify the most obvious cause. 'I slept because I was tired,' 'I asked a question because I was curious,' and whatever else. Nothing in this world is separate from anything else. There is no cause separate from other causes, no effect separate from other effects, and no cause separate from effect. Would you have this lesson consist of different words? You would have to re-arrange the First Swirlings of the universe to have a new lesson. Therefore, when we speak of a 'Why' or a 'Because,' it can only be a matter of expediency, not of truth. This is why it is said that reason is a lie, that there is a factor infinite and unknown, making all reason's words skew-wise.[280]

There is no 'Why' nor is there a 'Whence' or 'Whither.'[281] To ask 'Why' is to cause a Will to explain itself, but the Will does not need to explain itself; the Will simply does. To ask 'Why' is to cause a Will to justify itself, but the Will does not need to justify itself; the Will simply does. You cannot find where the action of a Master truly came from, nor can you find where the action of a Master will lead to.

The action of the Master is no different from the action of one who is yet to become a Master. All actions, from Master or not, are full of joy. Therefore: Rejoice!"

The sixth disciple moved back and the Master waited for the seventh disciple to approach. The seventh disciple merely stepped forward, took the Master's glass and took a large swig from it. The seventh disciple wiped her mouth, looked at the Master, smiled, and then belched.

The Master laughed and said:

"There is your true lecture for the day, spoken from the belly rather than the throat."

The seven disciples and the Master then rejoiced.

AUMGN. AUMGN. AUMGN.

CHAPTER 4:
THE PERFECTION OF UNDERSTANDING SUTRA

1   The noble Master V.V.V.V.V.,

2   while practicing the deep practice of the Perfection of Understanding,

3   conquered the Heavens and Earth by the power of Truth while living,

4   and, seeing the Heavens and Earth were but as shadows,

5   said, "Ha! Child of Earth,

6   Two is None, None is Two;

7   None is not separate from Two, Two is not separate from None;

8   whatever is Two is None, whatever is None is Two;

9   The same holds for memory, volition, emotion, reason, instinct, consciousness and sense.

10   Even now and here, Child of Earth, absolutely all things are of the nature of None:

11   they are neither born nor die, neither pure nor impure, neither increasing nor diminishing.

12   Therefore, Child of Earth, in the None there is no Two,

13   no memory, no volition, no emotion, no reason, no instinct, no consciousness, nor sense;

14 No eye, no ear, no nose, no tongue, no body and no mind;

15 No shape, no sound, no smell, no taste, no feeling and no thought;

16 No element of consciousness, from eye consciousness to conceptual consciousness;

17 No causal link, from ignorance to old age and death,

18 And no end of causal link, from ignorance to old age and death;

19 No Trance of Sorrow, no Knowledge and Conversation, no crossing of the Abyss, no Path;

20 No knowledge, no attainment, and no non-attainment.

21 Therefore, Child of Earth, without attainment,

22 Masters take refuge in the Perfection of Understanding

23 and live without space-marks.

24 Without space-marks and thus without fears,

25 They see through shadows and finally attainment.

26 All Masters past, present, and future

27 also take refuge in the Perfection of Understanding

28 and realize unsurpassed, perfect Understanding.

29 You should therefore know the great mantra of the Perfection of Understanding,

30 the mantra of great magick,

31 the unsurpassed mantra,

32 the mantra equal to that without equal,

33 which transcends all shadows and is True, not false,

34 the mantra in the Perfection of Understanding spoken thus:

35 'Gone, gone, gone beyond, gone completely beyond, hriliu ha.'"

CHAPTER 5:
A COMMENTARY ON
THE PERFECTION OF
UNDERSTANDING SUTRA

"I am identical with All and None."

–Liber V vel Reguli

"The Perfection of Understanding Sutra" is based on the "Heart Sutra," one of the most – if not *the* most – famous of the Mahayana Buddhist texts. Its full title is "The Heart of the Perfection of Wisdom" because it represents the "heart" or core of *prajnaparamita,* which is often translated as "the perfection of wisdom."

In Sanskrit, there is a difference made by some Buddhists between *jnana,* knowledge, and *prajna,* wisdom. *Jnana* refers to conventional knowledge whereas *prajna* refers to transcendent knowledge or wisdom. The term "Understanding" is used here because it has the connotation of this transcendent knowledge in our tradition. In the Qabalah, we distinguish between *Da'ath,* knowledge, and *Binah,* understanding; *Da'ath* is seen as the crown of the mind, or *ruach,* whereas *Binah* is above the Abyss, beyond the realm of duality, and the place of *neschamah,* which can be translated in many ways but essentially refers to this transcendent understanding.[282] The perfection of Understanding is therefore a perfection of this transcendent faculty or state.

This distinction between *jnana* and *prajna* – between *ruach* and *neschamah,* between knowledge and Understanding – is paralleled in the Two Truths doctrine of Buddhism that states there are two levels of truth: (1) the relative or conventional truth and (2) the absolute or ultimate Truth. For simplicity's sake, we might say that knowledge is composed of conventional truths and Understanding is ultimate truth. One must "keep separate the planes" – Understanding does not negate knowledge, and knowledge does not negate Understanding. We might say in terms of Understanding that "there is no difference between any one thing and any other thing" while we might simultaneously say in terms of knowledge that, for example, "fire is not the same as water." They are both true on their own "planes."[283]

Binah, or Understanding, is the Sephirah on the Tree of Life that corresponds to the Great Mother, called Babalon in our tradition. In this way, "Perfection of Understanding" is simply a name for Babalon, and vice versa. Further, the grade of "Magister

Templi" or "Master of the Temple" is attributed to this Sephirah, and one who attains to this grade is therefore identical with the Perfection of Understanding. One "becomes" a Master of the Temple by "crossing the Abyss" that separates the Supernal Triad from the rest of the Tree of Life; the process is only complete when one has drained all of one's blood – individuality or ego – into the Cup of Babalon.[284] One who has crossed is called "Nemo,"[285] which means "no man," because there is no ego, there is no "self" left. Only by a complete transcendence of the *ruach,* of the dualistic mind, can one come into the Womb of Babalon.

This Perfection of Understanding Sutra is, by its name, understood to be addressing the nature of Understanding. The aim is not to analyze, conceptualize, and categorize; the aim is to lead the mind of the aspirant to transcend itself, to abide in the Perfection of Understanding. In a way, the sutra is speaking "down" to the dualistic mind from the non-dual place of Understanding, and it may therefore seem to be paradoxical or even contradictory. As it is said, "And this is the great Mystery of the Supernals that are beyond the Abyss. For below the Abyss, contradiction is division; but above the Abyss, contradiction is Unity. And there could be nothing true except by virtue of the contradiction that is contained in itself."[286]

[182]

This sutra is, in brief, a text that expounds upon the Truth in Thelema of what is known as "0=2." It relates this Truth from the perspective of one who has attained to 0 or "None," one who is known as a Master (of the Temple). Its purpose is to declare this doctrine both succinctly and thoroughly, giving its implications in terms of theory and ending with a mantra that is given for practice.

As we may see: nothing in this sutra is new. All of these teachings can be found implicitly and explicitly in the corpus of Thelemic texts. Thelema is a syncretic philosophy, synthesizing the many truths of different traditions but all in the light of the Law of Liberty. This sutra conveys that same Truth already found within other Thelemic texts, but it is short, succinct, and beautiful; it allows us to climb the mountain of Truth from the Eastern slope, appreciating the same Truth, but from another approach. By gaining another perspective or lens on the same Truth, we may obtain a clearer and fuller appreciation of it. It is another opportunity to allow you, the reader, to achieve this Perfection of Understanding, to become a Master in your turn, by studying it, repeating it, chanting it, practicing it, and living it. A feast of unbounded life and joy is offered openly with these 35 lines, that you may smell it, be drawn to it, be sustained and inspired by it. Let us partake of it:

1 The noble Master V.V.V.V.V.,

The term "noble" is used (*arya* in the original Heart Sutra), and it refers firstly to one who is a King in the way the term is used throughout *The Book of the Law*. A King is one who is aware of his True Nature, a *bodhisattva,* which has been translated as "champion of enlightenment." Noble is a word that, etymologically, comes from the same root as *gnosis,* and therefore signifies one who has direct, experiential, transcendent knowledge, which is called Understanding within this text. As the Master Therion has said, "'the royal:' these are the men whose nature is kingly, the men who 'can.' They know themselves born rulers, whether their halidom be Art, or Science, or aught else soever."[287]

The term "Master" is used, and it has a technical sense of being the "Magister" or "Master of the Temple," i.e. one who has attained to the Sphere of Binah on the Tree of Life, having crossed the Abyss by draining out every last drop of blood of self. Also, a "master" is one who has mastered or perfected something, and this Master is the Perfection of Understanding. Further, "master" implies someone who is a "chief," and this Master is the "chief of all" of which the Master Therion has written "The chief, then, is he who has destroyed this sense of duality... it means that such an one is completely master of his universe."[288] The term "Master" is used here in place of *bodhisattva* that is used in the original text, which means "being or champion (*sattva*) of enlightenment (*bodhi*)." The essential meaning is identical to that implied by the term "Master."

The name "V.V.V.V.V." is now used, and this is the motto of the grade of Magister Templi, or Master of the Temple. It is thus proper to the nature of this text being the Perfection of Understanding. "V.V.V.V.V." stands for "Vi Veri Vniversus Vivus Vici," which translates to mean "By the power of Truth, I while living have conquered the Universe." This name is therefore proper to this text and this grade because the "Truth" is here identical with Understanding; the conquering of the Universe is attained through the Perfection of Understanding and it reflects the fact that V.V.V.V.V. is called "Master." This also shows that the name of this Master is also her nature. This is similar to the name used in the original text, "Avalokiteshvara," which means "Master who looks down," both a name and a description of the *bodhisattva*'s nature. Whosoever has the power of the Perfection of Understanding is worthy of being called V.V.V.V.V. Whosoever has the power of the Perfection of Understanding is a Master and has triumphed by Truth; they are crowned and conquering.[289]

2 **while practicing the deep practice of the Perfection of Understanding,**

The Master is practicing the practice, walking the walk. The Master is not talking about the deep practice or analyzing, criticizing, debating, discussing, conceptualizing, questioning, considering, doubting, justifying, or arguing about the practice. The Master is practicing the practice. The Master is doing, just as the Law is "Do what thou wilt" and nothing else. This simple but crucial fact is what separates the armchair magicians from the actual magicians. One must rise up in order to awake.[290] Not otherwise can one become a Master.

This practice is described as "deep" (*gambhira* in the original text). In one sense, this practice is deep as opposed to superficial. More importantly, the term "deep" (*gambhira*) is used in Sanskrit to describe the navel and the vagina. The navel is the place of the umbilical cord and symbolizes rebirth, just as the third penal sign of the Priest in the Gnostic Mass ends by touching this spot.[291] The vagina also refers to rebirth, specifically from the Womb of Babalon from which one arises as a Master of the Temple, a *bodhisattva*. The "Diamond Sutra" says, "From this is born the unexcelled, perfect enlightenment of *tathagatas, arhans,* and fully enlightened ones. From this are born *buddhas* and *bhagavans.*" This is the the Womb of the Perfection of Understanding, the City of the Pyramids, and nothing could be "deeper" than the womb of this Mystery of

Mystery; as it is said, She is the one womb wherein all men are begotten and wherein they shall rest.[292] In a different, longer version of the original "Heart Sutra," the Buddha's *samadhi* is called *gambhira avabhasan,* which translates to "Manifestation of the Deep" and refers once again to the entry into the Womb of Babalon, the Perfection of Understanding, and one's rebirth as a Master.

The "deep practice of the Perfection of Understanding" has no particular practice, though a mantra is given at the end of this text as a means to attain thereto. It is a deep *samadhi,* becoming Naught, yet these are merely words and do not clearly designate an accurate meaning. The Oath of becoming a Master includes swearing to understand all things, to love all things, to perform all things, to endure all things, to work without attachment, and to work in truth. A study of *Liber Cheth vel Vallum Abiegnus* is instructive in this matter,[293] as well as – as always – a close study of *The Book of the Law* where certain hints are given as to the path and the reward, so to speak. When Masters practice the Perfection of Understanding, they do not think "I am practicing the Perfection of Understanding" nor do they think "I am not practicing the Perfection of Understanding" nor do they think "I am not not practicing the Perfection of Understanding." And that is why they are Masters. Hath not the Master said, "It is not known if it be known"?[294] At the end of the Path, Masters awaken to the understanding that there was no person who cultivates nor a path that is cultivated.

conquered the Heavens and Earth by the power of Truth while living,

In the original text, the line reads "looked upon the Five Skandhas" and, as "Avalokiteshvara" means "Master who looks down," the *bodhisattva* practices the practices for which he was named. Likewise: the noble Master V.V.V.V.V. practices the practice for which the name "V.V.V.V.V." is given. That is, the Master conquers the Universe by the power of Truth while living.

Rather than the "Five Skandhas," which is a decidedly Buddhist teaching, the term "Heavens and Earth" are used. One could argue that the Five Elements are a parallel worth noting, but one could then believe that the Seven Planets were not included in the Master's deep Perfection of Understanding, but this is not so. One could also argue that "body and mind" are an English substitute for the Five Skandhas, yet one could argue that this leaves out the "external world" and this is not so.

"Heavens" here includes the entire Macrocosm: the seven classical Planets as symbolizing the workings of everything in the celestial sphere. "Earth" here includes the entire Microcosm: the Four Elements, both externally and internally. This distinction between Heavens and Earth is, like all things, a conventional and therefore arbitrary distinction.

The point is absolutely everything that we consider to exist is penetrated and conquered by the Truth of the Master's Perfection of Understanding. Nothing in the self or not-self, nothing in the ego or non-ego, nothing in the Microcosm or Macrocosm, nothing in the Heavens or Earth are exempt from this; they are equivalent to the entire Universe, every last particle of dust.[295] This includes consciousness itself. This conquering is not of a stronger overpowering a weaker; it is a a mastery; it is a penetration like the Lance of the Priest piercing the Veil of the Abyss to reveal the Limitless Light of the Perfection of Understanding.[296]

4 and, seeing the Heavens and Earth were but as shadows,

The original text reads, "And seeing they were empty of self existence." This is the fundamental insight of the Heart Sutra emptiness (*shunyata*). This is specifically the emptiness of self existence, meaning that nothing in the Heavens and Earth – or the Five Skandhas to use the original text's phrase – contain anything that is permanent, self-substantial, and independent. Nothing exists by itself or as itself, so everything is empty of self-existence. This is one of the Three Marks or Characteristics of all things, *anatta* in Pali or *anatman* in Sanskrit, which the Master Therion designated as the Word of Siddhartha the *buddha* as a Magus.[297] This is not overlooked in the New Aeon; as it is written, "All words are sacred and all prophets true; save only that they understand a little."[298]

"Seeing" refers to Understanding, as opposed to "not seeing" which is ignorance. When one's eyes are closed, one is darkness and when one's eyes are open, one sees the Light. These are simply metaphors to help point towards the import of this phrase, for – in another and exactly opposite sense – light can be seen as that which obscures or blinds (i.e. ignorance), being based on vibration or duality, and darkness (or "NOX") is true Understanding. This "seeing" is of the Eye in the Triangle, not the two eyes of duality.[299] Again: these are mere metaphors, signs pointing to the actual destination. As it has been said in our holiest Book, "There is great danger in me; for who doth not understand these runes shall make a great miss."[300]

The Heavens and Earth are seen to be "but as shadows." The reference is to *Liber AL,* II:9, "Remember all ye that existence is pure joy; that all the sorrows are but as shadows; they pass & are done; but there is that which remains." The statement that existence is pure joy flips the First Noble Truth of the Buddha on its head, though it does not negate the First Noble Truth. The First Noble Truth that "Existence is suffering" (as a poor translation) is still true for those looking up from below the Abyss, so to speak, and "existence is pure joy" is true for those looking down from above the Abyss.

The term "shadows" implies something ever-changing and unreal, an almost exact parallel of something being "empty of self-existence." It is an illusion, like the shadows cast on the walls of Plato's cave. Shadows are things that look like something real but are really nothing. The Master has said, "Sorrows, being thus errors of vision, not real in themselves, pass and are done as soon as the mind ceases to dwell on them."[301] This does not say that the Heavens and Earth do not exist at all, but the way in which we say they exist – the way in which we take them to be real – is a delusion.

The phrase "but as" implies that they are not literally shadows; it is, again, a metaphor. The injunction is not to knock away old beliefs and set up new beliefs in their place; the injunction is to practice the Perfection of Understanding. In short: Become a Master of the Temple! As the Master has said, "One must understand the Universe perfectly, and be utterly indifferent to its pressure. These are the virtues which constitute a Master of the Temple."[302]

In a way, this can be seen as the core of this sutra. The un-initiate – the ordinary person – takes the shadows for reality, thinking that the self and the world is real and permanent. In this way, the ordinary person clings to illusions, which pass and are done. Therefore, as Chen-k'o says, "Thus, they hear about life and are pleased. They hear about death and are distressed."[303] The Master sees the hurt that comes from failing to "bind nothing," and this Master knows there is also no one who suffers from these illusions, having eliminated the delusion of a separate self.[304] Once one realizes that everything in the Heavens and on Earth are but as shadows, the Veil of duality is pierced and one knows naught but Limitless Light.

5 said, "Ha! Child of Earth,

The first thing said is, "Ha!" The original text has the word "here" instead, coming from the Sanskrit *iha*. This is the exclamation of enlightenment, the raised finger of Gu-tei, the uplifted flower of Buddha.[305] The meaning of "here" also implies that enlightenment is available here and now. As it is written in our Holy Books, "This immortality is no vain hope beyond the grave: I offer you the certain consciousness of bliss. I offer it at once, on earth; before an hour hath struck upon the bell, ye shall be with Me in the Abodes that are beyond Decay."[306] "Ha!" is also an exclamation of joy, a spontaneous laugh, and therefore a proclamation of the Perfection of Understanding expressing itself in pure joy. It is also the final word of *The Book of the Law* and therefore implies a seal or consummation, a statement complete in itself. More esoterically, it is Heh-Aleph, enumerating to 6, the number of the Sun of enlightenment or illumination, the mystic number of Binah, the Womb of Babalon, the Perfection of Understanding Herself.[307]

The Master then addresses "Child of Earth." The original text had "Shariputra," which literally means "son of Shari," after his mother. In this way, a parallel is drawn where the Master is addressing the "son or child of Earth," with the Earth being his mother. And, of course, this Earth is Babalon, the Great Mother and the Perfection of Understanding, even as she is called the "one Earth, the mother of us all."[308] Further, the "Child of Earth" is a term used in the Golden Dawn Neophyte ceremony, symbolizing the early or material nature of natural man, one who comes from the darkness of Matter and strives toward the Light. This sutra is therefore addressed to anyone and everyone who is attempting to walk the Path to attain Truth.

ᵭ Two is None, None is Two;

The original text has one of the most famous lines of Mahayana Buddhism: "form is emptiness, emptiness is form." Re-translating this into terms used within the tradition of Thelema is no easy task. "Form" could be taken as anything seen as stable or permanent whereas "emptiness" could be seen as impermanence or change. Taken this way, it is then similar to the statement made by the Master, "And this understanding that Stability is Change, and Change Stability, that Being is Becoming, and Becoming Being, is the Key to the Golden Palace of this Law."[309] Yet this is not quite adequate, because "emptiness" implies emptiness of self-existence, as mentioned earlier. Something can, in theory, be constantly changing yet retain a fundamental self-existence, yet this is exactly what this line denies. "Form" is not merely stability, but includes all things that we think of as changing as well: it constitutes the entire Universe of which the ordinary person is aware and takes to be real; our "Two" or "All." "Emptiness" is not mere change, but more of being devoid of any kind of self-existence or divisibility or separation. It therefore

[194]

is more like our "None" or "Naught," the non-dual continuum whereof nothing may be spoken.

In light of this, to say "Two is None" – or "All is Naught" – is essentially to say that all things in the realm of multiplicity are actually not existent in themselves but truly Naught. In other words, 2 is 0. Duality turns out to be, in reality, Nothing. 0 merely appears as $1 + -1$ – as duality or 2 or multiplicity – to our deluded perception. This is a commonplace mystical truth across virtually all traditions: the world of duality or multiplicity is, in reality, a Unity which is called Naught in our tradition. As the Master has said, "By Light shall ye look upon yourselves, and behold All Things that are in Truth One Thing only, whose name hath been called No Thing... In this Light naught exists, for It is homogeneous: and therefore have men called it Silence, and Darkness, and Nothing. But in this, as in all other effort to name it, is the root of every falsity and misapprehension, since all words imply some duality. Therefore, though I call it Light, it is not Light, nor absence of Light. Many also have sought to describe it by contradictions, since through transcendent negation of all speech it may by some natures be attained. Also by images and symbols have men striven to express it: but always in vain."[310] This truth is also seen in the Qabalistic "key" of *The Book of the Law,* insofar as the Hebrew word for God "AL"

(Aleph-Lamed), implying "All" (or Two), is the same value as the word for nothing, "LA" (Lamed-Aleph), implying "None" (or Zero), and they are therefore identical from a certain perspective.[311]

Now, the real surprise comes, although it is logically implicit in the former statement: Naught is All. 2 is actually 0, and 0 is actually 2. With "Two is None" we recognize that the true nature of all things is actually "0," an ineffable and unconditioned Naught, yet with "None is Two" we assert that this All or 2 is actually the true nature of reality as well: its fundamental nature is None, and None appears as and is Two. The first clause (Two is None) asserts illusion to be reality in actuality, it is a rebuff to the ordinary person who takes the realm of multiplicity or All to be real. The second clause (None is Two) asserts reality as illusion, a rebuff to the lop-sided mystic who asserts that Naught is the only truth without realizing that the Two is not separate from Naught: 2 is 0, and 0 is 2; *samsara* is *nirvana,* and *nirvana* is *samsara*. The world of "Two," the realm of multiplicity, is empty of reality because nothing exists in itself, depending always on something, so we cannot claim the shadows of multiplicity do exist, yet we can not say that these shadows do not exist, because they exist as delusions, as expressions of Naught in Two. Everything is actually Naught, and Naught is actually

Everything. 2=0 and 0=2. Neither do the shadows exist nor do they not exist.

In Thelema, we accept the appearance of the illusion of duality, the shadows that pass and are done, as a fact of reality, so to speak. We do not fall into the mystic trap of denying duality to achieve non-duality, calling the realm of Two – or multiplicity or All – mere evil or illusion; this "evil" of duality is merely a conventional truth. This would set up the unhealthy duality of None versus Two, non-duality versus duality. The Naught figures itself or is apprehended as Two to know and experience the possibilities of Itself, and this Two is nothing other than the Naught. The None is "divided for love's sake, for the chance of union,"[312] and yet this Two is ultimately None. The Naught does not create a Two separate from itself: the Two is Its very body. The true nature of Two is itself Naught and Naught is that Two. Inside 0 there is no 2, and outside 2 there is no 0. Bodhidharma said, "You might think you can find a *buddha* or enlightenment somewhere beyond the mind, but such a place doesn't exist... Beyond this mind you'll never see a *buddha*... The mind is the *buddha*, and *buddha* is the mind. Beyond the mind there's no *buddha*, and beyond the *buddha* there's no mind."[313] The doctrine is essentially equivalent. As Nagarjuna says, "Emptiness and form share the same nature" and Ching-chueh explains, "Hence, they are said to be 'not separate.'"[314] The Master has said, "Nuit is that which is equally 0 & 2. This Equation 0=2 the Master-Key of the Understanding of the Nature of the Universe."[315] Because words tend toward obscurity and misapprehension, the virtue of Silence is praised by virtually all mystics and is the proper attitude of a Master of the Temple.

7 None is not separate from Two, Two is not separate from None;

It is theoretically feasible that something can be something else at a certain point but not at others; they can overlap but not completely coincide. For example, salt is one with water in the ocean but it is possible to extract the salt therefrom in a separate form. Or, as an another example, we might say "Bob is happy," but that doesn't mean that Bob is always happy – the two terms "Bob" and "happy" coincide but are not necessarily identical. This line asserts that Naught and All, 0 and 2, are not only identical, they are not different in any kind or way or form; they are indistinguishable. There are no cases where Two is different or separate from None and there are no cases where None is different or separate from Two.

How silly it would be to set up a new duality between None and Two! A person in *samsara*, the world of Two – the world below the Abyss, of All, of multiplicity – strives to create the boat of Adeptship through Magick and Mysticism to arrive at the other shore, i.e. attain *nirvana*, the world of Naught – the world above the Abyss, of indivisibility, of non-duality. Yet, in crossing "to the other shore" one realizes that it is the same shore – there is no "other shore," nor is there a boat, nor is there anyone who ever attained: these are all shadows. Thus it is said that *nirvana* is *samsara*, however displeasing that is to those still grasping after shadows.

8 whatever is Two is None, whatever is None is Two;

This reinforces the idea of the previous lines, asserting that 2 is 0 and 0 is 2; they are identical regardless of how either are conceived. The non-existence of Two is not denied (for Two is None), nor is it asserted (for None is Two); likewise, the existence of Two is not denied (for None is Two), nor is it asserted (for Two is None).

For one below the Abyss, their work is to realize that Two is None, uniting opposites in love under will to annihilate both and achieve the non-dual Silence. For one above the Abyss, their work is o realize that None is Two, expressing their non-duality in duality or the possibility of experience. For the former there is *solve* and for he latter there is *coagula*.[316] As the Master has said, "I destroyed all hings; they are reborn in other shapes. I gave up all for One; this One hath given up its Unity for all"[317] and "The Many is as adorable o the One as the One is to the Many. This is the Love of These; creation-parturition is the Bliss of the One; coition-dissolution is the Bliss of the Many."[318] Ordinary people see Two but they don't see None; mystics see None but they don't see Two. The Master, practicing the Perfection of Understanding, knows that Two is None and None is Two, None is not separate from Two and Two is not eparate from None, and that whatever is Two is None and whatever s None is Two.

) The same holds for memory, volition, emotion, reason, instinct, consciousness and sense.

The original text read "the same holds for sensation and perception, memory and consciousness," an exposition of the four Skandhas other than form also being part of the same equation. Here, we have memory, volition, emotion, reason, instinct, consciousness, and sense. These are the seven Sephiroth below the

Abyss: Chesed (memory), Geburah, (volition), Netzach (emotion), Hod (reason), instinct (Yesod), consciousness (Tiphareth), and sense (Malkuth). In this way, nothing in the realm of Two – of multiplicity, of everything below the Abyss – is excluded. All things within the Universe – the Heavens and Earth – are part of this equation of 0=2. Memory, volition, emotion, reason, instinct, and consciousness are specifically aspects of the mind, and sense is the material world including the body.

Everything that we think of as ourselves is, in fact, not our self – it is partial, co-dependent, ever-changing, having no substance or subsistence in itself. To use a phrase, our "True Self" cannot be found in any of these things. This includes "volition" – our so-called "willpower" – and consciousness or awareness itself. Yet, in another sense, our True Self can be found in all of these things. This Two is actually None, and the None is shown by this Two. None is not merely shown by Two, it *is* it. This is why the Master is able to claim, "I am clothed with the body of flesh" at the same time as he claims, "I am one with the Eternal and Omnipotent God."[319] This is why the Master is able to claim, "I am identical with All and None. I am in All and all in me; I am, apart from all and lord of all, and one with all."[320]

Thus, those striving for something other than what is are deluded; in this way, there is no wisdom and there is no attainment. Our holiest Book says, "There is none that shall be cast down or lifted up: all is ever as it was"[321] and the Master has said, "Initiation means the Journey Inwards: nothing is changed or can be changed; but all is trulier understood with every step."[322]

10 **Even now and here, Child of Earth, absolutely all things are of the nature of None,**

"Even now and here" is a translation of *iha,* which means "here" and is translated as "Ha!" before, yet this time meaning would be lost if there was not the implication that, even at this moment in time and point in space, Two is None. Even as the Master has said, "Thou Child, holy Thy name and undefiled! Thy reign is come: Thy will is done. Here is the Bread; here is the Blood. Bring me through midnight to the Sun! Save me from Evil and from Good! That Thy one crown of all the Ten even now and here be mine. AMEN." The reign *is* come, the will *is* done, and the one crown (Naught) of all the Ten (All) belongs to the Master *even now and here*. This is the same doctrine given in *The Gospel of Thomas* where it is written, "His disciples said to him: 'On what day will the kingdom come?' [Jesus said:] 'It will not come when it is expected.

[202]

No one will say: 'See, it is here!' or: 'Look, it is there!' but the Kingdom of the Father is spread over the earth and men do not see it.'" Even so, the Sun is always shining though we may not perceive It, and Hadit is always at the core of every person, though we may not know Him.[323]

"Absolutely all things" is used in place of "all dharmas." "Dharmas" here essentially means anything whatsoever that is taken as real. The implication is that one might think that, beyond the Five Skandhas (or the Heavens and the Earth), there may *dharmas* that are not subject to this same emptiness of self-existence. This line shows that everything and all their sub-sets and categories and expressions are of the nature of None: indivisible, inseparable, ineffable.

To state that "absolutely all things are of the nature of None" is to say that all possible things, summarized by the term "All" or "Two," are defined by their true nature being Naught. Fa-tsang says succinctly, "It means without duality."[324] This means there is no one who knows, there is nothing known, and there is no knowledge. There is no one who attains, there is nothing attained, and there is no attainment. Because there is no knowledge, there is likewise no ignorance; because there is no attainment, there is likewise no non-attainment. The mind reels at such statements, and this is why this is he Perfection of Understanding and not the Perfection of Knowledge.

11 they are neither born nor die, neither pure nor impure, neither ncreasing nor diminishing.

All things' true nature is Naught or Nothingness. This Naught s neither born nor dies. Since nothing in the world of Two has self-existence in itself – there is no difference – then impermanence does 1ot apply. It is for this reason that the pure soul is said to be "individual" – that is, it is not "dividual" or divided.[325] This Naught 1either enters into existence nor exits into non-existence, and herefore it is neither born nor does it die. Only from the perspective of Two is there anything in the category of time, yet, None being peyond this category, nothing begins or ends and therefore it is said o be of the nature of None. It is for this reason that the pure soul is said to be "eternal"[326] and it is for this reason None is called the 3ornless One.[327]

This Naught or 0 is neither pure nor defiled. There is no suffering nor joy in the ordinary sense of the terms.[328] Suffering comes from taking the shadows of the world of Two to be real, i.e. comes from attachment (in Buddhist terminology) to these shadows since they inevitably pass and are done. For convenience's sake, we say that ordinary man is defiled and must, through a series of steps or grades or degrees, remove these defilements or this ignorance to become pure. Nonetheless, everything's true nature is Naught, our distinction between things being mere convention and illusion. Purity requires a notion of impurity, being defiled a notion of being undefiled, but all things are of the same nature, being ultimately None, and therefore purity and defilement are delusions. There is no one who suffers or enjoys, there is nothing suffered or enjoyed, and there is no suffering or enjoyment. With Hui-neng we may ask, "Where did you get this dust?" Or: Where did you get this suffering or enjoyment? Who is suffering or enjoying? Where did you get this question? Who is asking this question? These are, of course, rhetorical questions implying that the answer in all cases is "Nowhere" or "No one" or, simply, None.

There is nothing that is truly increasing or diminishing, for nothing in the realm of Two is self-sufficient or self-existent, always depending on everything else. Since all things are empty in this way, they are not "complete," and since nothing in them can truly be distinguished as a part or a whole, they are not incomplete or deficient. The nature of an un-initiate (one with diminished knowledge) and initiate (one with increased knowledge) are ultimately the same, being of the nature of Nothingness; "I am perfect, being Not."[329] With this we do not merely claim that Malkuth is in Kether and Kether in Malkuth, we claim Malkuth *is* Kether and Kether *is* Malkuth. Though this may in one sense be revolutionary it is, in another sense, nothing new. All is ever as it was and ever as it will be. Bodhidharma says, "This mind, through endless aeons without beginning, has never varied. It has never lived or died, appeared or disappeared, increased or decreased. It is not pure or impure, good or evil, past or future. It is not true or false. It is not male or female. It does not appear as a monk or a layman, an elder or a novice, a sage or a fool, a *buddha* or a mortal. It strives for no realization and suffers no karma. It has no strength or form. It is like space. You cannot possess it and you cannot lose it."[330]

What follows is essentially a list of "absolutely all things," using various lists based on certain Buddhist categories – the Five Skandhas and the Eighteen Elements of Perception – in order to exhaust the possibility of thinking anything is exempt from being defined by Naught as its true nature.

2 **Therefore, Child of Earth, in the None there is no Two,**

13 no memory, no volition, no emotion, no reason, no instinct, no consciousness, nor sense;

The focus now becomes "in the None," so we come to see the Zero-perspective, so to speak. The None is beyond duality, the Two, and therefore beyond all positive assertions and all categories insofar as these things distinguish one thing from another thing. Because there is no time, there is no start nor finish, no birth nor death. Because there is no space, there is no here nor there, no inside nor outside. Because there is no causality, there is no cause nor effect. The fundamental nature of Two is not birth or death, purity or impurity, increasing or diminishing, change or stability; the fundamental nature of all things is None, an indivisible continuity of which naught may be spoken.

In the None, no Two can be found, thus it says "no Two." Likewise, no memory can be found, no volition, no emotion, no reason, no instinct, no consciousness, nor sense. The entire Tree of Life below the Abyss is seen to be nothing but a convenient fiction, yet it is a fiction that convinces most of its reality. They do not exist in themselves as discrete or self-subsisting entities, thus we say "in the None there is no Two." In the Perfection of Understanding, there is no trace of any of these things: it is not that they do not exist nor that they are annihilated, both of which set up a duality of existence and non-existence; it is that their fundamental nature is Nothingness. As the Master has said, "That is not which is. The only Word is Silence. The only Meaning of that Word is not. Thoughts are false."[331]

14 No eye, no ear, no nose, no tongue, no body and no mind;

Just to make sure that nothing is excluded, various lists are given, all of which are denied reality or self-sufficiency in themselves in the light of the None. The Buddhist conception of the senses includes a sixth sense of mind that receives the impressions of thought just as the eye receives impressions of sight, the tongue receives impressions of taste, *et cetera*.

In the None, nothing exists in and by itself, for all divisions of things from each other is simply a delusion. Thus our holiest Book declares, "Bind nothing! Let there be no difference made among you between any one thing & any other thing; for thereby there cometh hurt."[332] To say we have no eye in the None is not to say that we have no eyes but that eyes are not ultimately or fundamentally real in themselves; they are but as shadows in themselves and their true nature is None. Hui-ching says, "Although the nature of the eye is empty, it is not the case that there is no eye. This is also true of the other senses."[333] All of these sense organs treated as distinct and discrete entities is merely a convenient fiction that we are accustomed to believing; we treat them as self-sufficient and real when they are truly but as shadows. One Saint of our Gnostic Church, Friedrich Nietzsche, has said, "We have arranged for ourselves a world in which we can live – by positing bodies, lines, planes, causes and effects, motion and rest, form and content; without these articles of faith nobody could now endure life. But that does not prove them. Life is no argument. The conditions of life might include error."[334] Even a Westerner with no formal training in Magick or Meditation may catch glimpses of this Perfection of Understanding!

15 No shape, no sound, no smell, no taste, no feeling and no thought;

Each of the sensory organs mentioned in the previous line has certain sensory functions or realms of sensing. The previous line deals with the aspects of the sensorium and this line deals with various stimuli. The eye perceives shape, the ear perceives sound, the nose perceives smell, the tongue perceives taste, the body perceives feeling, and the mind perceives thought.

Just as the organs have no self-existent reality in themselves, neither do their domains or objects of perception. Every organ and their objects of perception are fundamentally of the nature of Naught. If reality is seamless and indivisible, a continuous and unbroken fabric, then any distinction of one thing from another is delusion, a mere convenient fiction that we use to navigate the world of Two that has no ultimate reality in itself. This includes both the eye and any possible shapes, the nose and any possible smells, *et cetera.*

16 No element of consciousness, from eye consciousness to conceptual consciousness;

The Master has said, "Consciousness results from the conjunction of a mysterious stimulus with a mysterious sensorium."[335] The 14th line dealt with the six types of sensorium (eye, ear, nose, tongue, body, and mind) and the 15th line dealt with the six types of stimulus (shape, sound, smell, taste, feeling, and thought). Together, these things create six types of consciousness: eye consciousness, ear consciousness, nose consciousness, tongue consciousness, body consciousness, and mind consciousness or "conceptual consciousness" as it is described here. Although only the first and last of these are mentioned in this line, all six are implied. The six sense faculties (or internal bases), six sense objects (or external bases), and six sense consciousnesses are, all together, everything of which we can possibly be aware – they are sometimes called the "Eighteen Dhatus" or the "Eighteen Elements of Perception."

When meditating upon these eighteen elements of perception in the Perfection of Understanding, all of them are seen to be empty of self-existence. They are all co-dependent and co-defined, and they are therefore not real in themselves. Their true nature, when penetrated, is Naught or Zero. No true self can be found in any of these elements separately or in conjunction, even though they compose the entire universe of which we are aware. One can say, for the sake of convenience, that the True Self is Naught, but this may lead easily into error for there is no distinction between anything self and anything not-self in this Truth. We may call it Truth, but this may lead easily into error for there is no distinction between truth and falsity in this None. We may call it None, but this may lead easily into error for there is no distinction between nothing and something. We may call it Silence, but this may lead easily into error for there is no distinction between silence and speech in this Nameless. We may call it Nameless, but this may lead easily into error for there is no distinction between nameless and named in This. We may call it This, but this may lead easily into error for here is no distinction between this and that in It. This is why speech s false, and this is why thought is false. Nonetheless, It is revealed in all speech and all thought, in all named and all nameless, in all speech and all silence, in all that is not and all that is, in all that is false and all that is true, in all that is self and all that is not-self, *et cetera*. That is why it is said Two is None and None is Two. Mystery of Mystery, indeed.

Lest we think this is a Truth of Buddhism and not of Thelema, the exact same Truth is spoken by our Master, identified with the None and speaking with the voice of the Child, crowned and conquering, immortal and sinless, free and unbounded: "I am light, and I am night, and I am that which is beyond them. I am speech, and I am silence, and I am that which is beyond them. I am life, and I am death, and I am that which is beyond them. I am war, and I am peace, and I am that which is beyond them. I am weakness, and I am strength, and I am that which is beyond them. Yet by none of these can man reach up to me. Yet by each of them must man reach up to me."[336]

7 **No causal link, from ignorance to old age and death,**

8 **And no end of causal link, from ignorance to old age and death;**

These causal links are a reference to the Twelve Links or Chains (*nidanas*) of Dependent Origination. These Twelve Links are ignorance that leads to mental formations that leads to consciousness that leads to name-and-form that leads to the six sense-gates that lead to contact that leads to feeling that leads to craving that leads to clinging that leads to becoming that leads to birth that leads to old age/death. Again, only the first (ignorance) and last (old age and death) are mentioned here for convenience but all are implied. It should be understood that the Twelve Links links do not simply go one way; they go back and forth and around and around, perpetuating our suffering in the delusion of *samsara* where we take the Two to be the only reality, grasping after shadows.

In the light of the Perfection of Understanding, causal links are, in truth, Naught. Philosophically, causation requires a cause separate from an effect. Seeing as how all Eighteen Elements of Perception were empty of reality and self-existence, all being intertwined and co-dependent, there is no true distinction between any one thing and any other thing. Cause and effect is therefore unreal as well except as a convenient fiction used to describe, explain, and function in the world. There is nothing in itself that is a cause nor anything in itself that is an effect, nor is there any self separate from any not-self that can be a cause or an effect.

Since these do not truly exist in the first place, there is no creation of causal links. Since these links are never created, there is no need to end – to destroy or dissolve – what never existed. All these things never began nor will they ever end; it is mere delusion that takes things as real and sees their beginning and their end. Because of true Nothingness, nothing can rise or fall, begin or end, be born or die. The Master does not confound the space-marks, nor does she confound the time-marks, nor does she confound the causality-marks, and thus is she worthy to be called Master.

19 No Trance of Sorrow, no Knowledge and Conversation, no crossing of the Abyss, no Path;

Now we pass to the subject of the Path of Attainment. The original text has the line "no suffering, no source, no relief, no path," which refers to the Four Noble Truths. This is altered to be resonant with the language of the Path in the Thelemic tradition. Within this tradition, there is a Trance or Vision of Sorrow that impels people to the Path. It is essentially coterminous with the realization of the First Noble Truth of Buddhism that existence is suffering (again, a poor translation, but used for convenience). In this, we realize that nothing we can think, say, or do will remove us from the dualistic world of impermanence. There is nothing substantial that can or will last, and all is condemned to the grave. Having analyzed all of the Eighteen Elements of Perception, we realize that they have no subsistence in themselves nor is there any self therein.

If all of these things are None in their true nature, if nothing ever was born or died, then there is, in reality, no self that ever suffered or endured the Trance of Sorrow. There never was a self that may arise as an Adept and attains to Knowledge and Conversation of the Holy Guardian Angel. There never was a self that can be annihilated in the crossing of the Abyss. As Hui-ching says, "If there is someone who can practice, then there must be a path to practice. But there is no person and no path, for both individuals and *dharmas* [all things] are empty."[337] Bodhidharma said, "If you attain anything at all, it is conditional, it is subject to *karma*. It results in retribution. It turns the Wheel. And as long as you are subject to birth and death, you will never attain enlightenment. To attainment enlightenment you have to see your nature. Unless you see your nature, all this talk about cause and effect is nonsense. *Buddhas* don't practice nonsense. A *buddha* is free of karma, free of cause and effect. To say he attains anything at all is to slander a *buddha*."[338]

20 No knowledge, no attainment, and no non-attainment.

Knowledge requires a relation between two things; for example, "leaves are green" establishes a relation between "leaves" and "green." Knowledge further requires a relation between a knower and a thing that is known. Since, in the light of None, all these things are seen to be unreal though convenient fictions, there is no knowledge. The Master has said, "Daäth—Knowledge—is not a Sephira. It is not on the Tree of Life: that is, there is in reality no such thing... the attempt to analyse the idea leads immediately to a muddle of the mind. But this is of the essence of the Occult Wisdom concerning Daäth. For Daäth is the crown of the Ruach, the Intellect; and its place is in the Abyss. That is, it breaks into pieces immediately when it is examined. There is no coherence below the Abyss, or in it; to obtain this, which is one of the chief canons of Truth, we must reach Neschamah."[339] Thus it is said there is "no knowledge."

Since there is no self to be found in any of the Eighteen Elements of Perception, there is no one to attain, nor is there anyone to not attain. The Path is only a valid exposition to one who lives in the world of Two, and, upon attaining the Perfection of Understanding in None, will realize that Two is None and None is Two. Yet None is not a state to be attained, for that implies attainment and the possibility of non-attainment, which are denied.

There was never a Path, nor was there knowledge, nor attainment, nor non-attainment. Two is None, always was, always is, and always will be. Ignorance of this is None, and Understanding of this is None. Thus it is said there is "no attainment" and "no non-attainment."

None is the only true reality, and it is already perfect, already pure, already Truth. Bodhidharma says, "The Way is basically perfect. It does not require perfecting."[340] The Master has said, "The soul is, in its own nature, perfect purity, perfect calm, perfect silence... This soul can never be injured, never marred, never defiled"[341] and "Nothing is changed or can be changed; but all is trulier understood with every step."[342] In this way, there is no cultivation of virtue nor accumulation of wisdom nor is there initiation. What is there to seek? Who is there to seek anything? In this way, there is no Path.

This line concludes the analysis of all parts of existence of which we are aware.

21 **Therefore, Child of Earth, without attainment,**

The previous nine lines outlined the nature and constituents of what we consider reality in the light of None. These next lines outline the career of a Master, so to speak.

In the traditional understanding, the Path ends with no "rebirth" insofar as the ego has been completely annihilated. In terms of Buddhism, the aspirant has escaped or been liberated from the Wheel of *samsara.* In contrast, the Path of the Master "ends" with no birth insofar as the Perfection of Understanding entails the realization that nothing ever came into existence in the first place and therefore nothing needs to be annihilated. Because nothing is annihilated, there is nothing impermanent about or for which we may suffer in the "realm of Two," so to speak. Because there is no Two, there is no need of liberation from Two. Because there is no need of liberation from Two, all beings are already freed from Two. Because all beings are already freed from Two, the Master has already accomplished the task of liberating all beings, the vow of all *bodhisattvas.* Because the vow to liberate all beings is fulfilled, Masters are liberated from liberating all beings. Thus we see that the fulfillment of the vow to enter back into the realm of Two in order to tend the garden" of disciples that they may attain is fulfilled when the Master is liberated from the concept of "beings" as distinct entities as well as being liberated from the notion of attainment itself. There are no separate beings in None and, having practiced the deep practice of the Perfection of Understanding, the Master ha

already fulfilled and been liberated from this task. It may be said

that it takes trillions of aeons for all beings to be liberated, yet the

Master asks, "What aeons? What liberation? What beings? Who said

this? Who answers?" The Master is in a place where the term

attainment and non-attainment have lost all meaning.

The vow of a Master, or the *bodhisattva* vow, is to attain

Understanding and to liberate all beings from their mis

understanding. Yet in becoming a Master, one could not possibly

take this vow for there are no beings to liberate and the notion of

attainment or liberation has lost all meaning. In achieving the vow, it

is discarded as delusion. The Master therefore disavows all vows as a

final vow.

22 Masters take refuge in the Perfection of Understanding

Buddhists traditionally take refuge in *buddha, dharma,* and

sangha. That is, they take refuge in the teacher (Buddha), the

teaching (*dharma*), and the community of those who follow this

teaching (*sangha*). These are the Three Refuges, also known as the

Three Jewels or Three Treasures. We see in this line, though, that

the Masters take refuge only in the Perfection of Understanding

Masters know that all teachers are, in their true nature, Naught; Masters know that all teachings, even all things, are truly Naught; Masters know that there are no separate beings to be taught, their true nature all being Naught. Masters take refuge, therefore, in the Perfection of Understanding, abiding in the None as the undivided, seamless continuum of true reality.

Our holiest Book says, "Nu is your refuge."[343] This is simply another way to say that Masters take refuge in the Perfection of Understanding. The Master has said, "The infinite unity is our refuge, since if our consciousness by in that unity, we shall care nothing for the friction of its component parts."[344] And this "infinite unity" is exactly that None of which has been spoken yet of which nothing can truly be spoken. Does not our holiest Book also say, "O Nuit, continuous one of Heaven, let it be ever thus; that men speak not of Thee as One but as None; and let them speak not of thee at all, since thou art continuous!"[345]

23 and live without space-marks.

The original text has the line "and live without walls of the mind." This is substituted out for "space-marks," for it is written in our holiest Book, "Bind nothing! Let there be no difference made among you between any one thing & any other thing; for thereby there cometh hurt... If this be not aright; if ye confound the space-marks, saying: They are one; or saying, They are many... then expect the direful judgments of Ra Hoor Khuit!"[346] There is no difference made, for all is None in the continuum we sometimes call Nu or Nuit.

Masters do not attribute reality to anything in combination as "one" or severally as "many." The Master has said, "But distinctions must not be made before Nuit, either intellectually, morally, or personally. Metaphysics, too, is intellectual bondage; avoid it! Otherwise one falls back to the Law of Hoor [that of the war of duality] from the perfect emancipation of Nuit. This is a great mystery, only to be understood by those who have fully attained Nuit and her secret Initiation."[347] That is, it is only to be Understood in the Perfection of Understanding that is but a name of Nuit and one who abides in the understanding thereof. It can be described, for the sake of convenience, as an object without a subject or a subject without an object. As an object without a subject, it is Nuit; as a subject without an object, it is Hadit. As an object without a subject, a Yogi may call it Brahman; as a subject without an object, a Yogi may call it Atman. Even as Atman is Brahman and Thou art That, Hadit and Nuit are both Perfect, being None. As our holiest

Book says, "The Perfect and the Perfect are one Perfect and not two; nay, are none!"[348]

24 Without space-marks and thus without fears,

To live without space-marks is to be liberated from all fear. If one lives without any distinction between any one thing and any other thing, what could possibly cause fear? Our holiest Book says, "Dost thou fail? Art thou sorry? Is fear in thine heart? Where I am these are not."[349] The Master has said, "This brings out what is a fact in psychology, the necessary connection between fear, sorrow, and failure... If one have a right apprehension of the Universe, if he know himself free, immortal, boundless, infinite force and fire, then may he will and dare. Fear, sorrow and failure are but phantoms. Hadit is everywhere; fear, sorrow, and failure are only 'shadows.'"[350]

One might say that fear begins with and is only possible in Two and it therefore ends in None, which is true at the conventional level. Yet in the None, one sees that it never arose and therefore will never cease; there was never birth and never will there be death. It is seen as a shadow that was never real in the first place.

It is only by establishing "space-marks," by asserting a reality in the difference between anything and anything else, that we have fear, sorrow, and failure. And does not our holiest Book say this clearly? "Bind nothing! Let there be no difference made among you between any one thing & any other thing; *for thereby there cometh hurt.*"[351] The Master has said, "Nuit is Space beyond the idea of Limit or Measure; She is also All Points of View no less than All Vistas seen therefrom. Bind nothing, for all things alike pertain to her, and her Nature is to compose All in One and Naught. One thing is in the end like all the rest; the seeming not alike comes as a dream from choosing images after one's own heart to worship them; thus each, though true as one of the All, is false if thought of as one apart from the rest."[352]

Fear, sorrow, and failure can only be within the realm of Two. If one desires a certain outcome but expects there may be another, there will be fear. If the undesired outcome arrives, there will be failure. Once this undesired outcome comes to pass, there is sorrow over this failure. There is therefore, as the Master says, "a necessary connection between fear, sorrow, and failure" that characterizes the psychology of one stuck in the realm of Two. If one does not attribute solidity and reality to the ever-changing shadows of Two, where is the fear of criticism? Where is the fear of embarrassment? Where is the fear of living a bad life? Where is the fear of failure? Where is the fear of death itself? Without space

arks, one lives without fears. By the power of the Truth of the
erfection of Understanding, one conquers the Universe while living.

5 They see through shadows and finally attainment.

Masters "see through" shadows, meaning they understand
their essentially illusory and unreal nature. Masters understand that
the fundamental nature of all things is None.

The original text says "they see through delusions and finally
nirvana." The traditional approach of mystics is to transcend
samsara, the world of Two, and seek *nirvana,* the world of None.
They seek to transcend the impermanent and seek the permanent,
they seek to transcend existence and seek non-existence, they seek to
transcend the impure and seek the pure.

The *bodhisattva* overcomes the delusion of attainment of
nirvana itself; the Master overcomes the attainment of the None
self. This None is not separate from Two; Two is None and None is
Two, as has been said repeatedly. Attainment is what we strive for,
and we walk the Path to achieve None, yet the final delusion is
attainment itself. Masters conquer this final delusion. If we see None
as permament or impermanent, we are not Masters; if we see None

as eternal or temporal, we are not Masters; if we see None as perfect or imperfect, we are not Masters.

Transcending all space-marks, the None is neither this nor that and it is both this and that. None is not something attained, it is the fundamental nature of all things, it is the ground of Two. Masters have seen through the shadow of None itself, and that is why they are called Masters. This is why it is said there is "no attainment," "no non-attainment," and "no Path."

26 All Masters past, present, and future

27 also take refuge in the Perfection of Understanding

Instead of the Three Refuges of *dharma* (teaching), *buddha* (teacher), and *sangha* (taught), instead of even taking refuge in the None as distinct from Two, Masters take refuge in the Perfection of Understanding. Because they live without space-marks, ever between Two and None, they abide in the Perfection of Understanding.

All Masters past, present, and future take refuge in this Perfection of Understanding because it is beyond all beginning and ending and beyond all cause and effect. In this Perfection of

Understanding, all Masters are eternally present and presently eternal.

28 and realize unsurpassed, perfect Understanding.

V.V.V.V.V. speaks with the language of conventional truth to explain the importance of the Perfection of Understanding. This is called "unsurpassed" because all other goals are seen as shadows beside the Perfection of Understanding. It is called "perfect" because all other goals are imperfect shadows beside it, and that is why it is the Perfection of Understanding. This Perfection of Understanding is beyond all striving and not-striving, it is beyond all goals and goal-lessness, it is beyond all attainment and non-attainment. Because it surpasses all of these conditions, we may only use dualistic language to point to it and call it "unsurpassed." Because it is perfect in light of all these imperfect conditions, we may only use dualistic language to point to it and call it "perfect."

29 You should therefore know the great mantra of the Perfection of Understanding,

We are told that we should "know" this great mantra, but this mantra is not an object of knowledge. This mantra involves no knowledge; if it is knowledge at all, it is the knowledge that leads beyond knowledge. In this way it is not knowledge. This is the only form of knowledge cultivated by a Master and the only knowledge worth knowing because it is not knowledge at all.

This is the great mantra of the Perfection of Understanding because it is the essential teaching of the Perfection of Understanding. Chanting this mantra does not bring power, it does not bring knowledge, it does not bring peace, it does not bring increase of anything at all. If one were to understand this mantra, one would be freed from all delusion, living without space-marks, and be rightfully called a Master. Yet, if one were to be a Master, one would not need a mantra to attain anything. It would be seen that there is nothing to be attained and nothing to not be attained. For those who do not have this sight, it is a lens to help focus one's vision. Once one crosses a river with a raft, one does not need a raft, and once you understand the mantra, you do not need the mantra.

30 the mantra of great magick,

The original text reads, "the mantra of great magic," and the addition of a "k" to the word "magic" brings new meaning in the light of Thelema. Magick is defined as the Science and Art of causing Change in conformity with Will, yet this is a special class of magick. Magick works through Will to cause change, and the nature of Will is Love, or union. All typical acts of Love or change simply lead to more acts of Love and change: they are still within Two, still within *samsara*. In this way, this is not mere magick to attain some end through change, but the magick of Love wherein all opposites are annihilated in perfect *samadhi*, perfect absorption or Love, so that That which transcends these opposites is seen: the Two is seen as None. In this way, it is a "change" only insofar as one moves beyond change and changelessness. Therefore it is not mere magick but "great magick."

If magick in the normal sense "gives birth" to something new, a new circumstance or experience, this great magick gives birth to a Master. This mantra of great magick is therefore the Perfection of Understanding itself, the Great Mother Babalon who gives birth to a Master of the Temple. Yet to say "gives birth" implies a beginning, something before and after, and we know that Masters transcend all space-marks and all time-marks as delusory shadows. This mantra of great magick therefore gives birth to the birthless, it causes the causeless, and that is why it is "great magick" and not mere magick, even though words, as always, fail us in describing it.

31 **the unsurpassed mantra,**

32 **the mantra equal to that without equal,**

This mantra of great magick is "unsurpassed," even as the Perfection of Understanding is unsurpassed. This mantra is unsurpassed because it goes beyond all categories. There is nothing surpassing it, there is nothing beyond it, and therefore it *is* the beyond, it *is* Nothing.

That without equal is the Perfection of Understanding, the Master herself. Because this mantra is identical with the Master, with the None, it is "equal to that without equal." Absolutely nothing in any of the categories mentioned in previous lines reaches up to equal this None; there is nothing below, above, or beside it. This is why Hadit claims, "I am alone."[353]

33 **which transcends all shadows and is True, not false,**

This mantra is given to them that still wander in the shadow-realm of Two, and it is therefore told to all aspirants that it "transcends all shadows." Its very nature is None and therefore transcends all shadows even though a Master who abides in None knows that it is identical with Two. We are told to cross from the shore of *samsara* to the other shore of *nirvana* but upon reaching this other shore, we come to understand that it is the same shore; *nirvana* is *samsara,* None is Two.

We are told that it is "True, not false" because it transcends all falsity that encompasses all the true and false of conventional truth. All truth and falsity of which we are aware is false in the light of the Truth of the Perfection of Understanding, embodied in the Masters and the mantra of great magick.

34 the mantra in the Perfection of Understanding spoken thus:

35 'Gone, gone, gone beyond, gone completely beyond, hriliu ha.'"

This mantra is "in" the Perfection of Understanding, even as the Master is in the Womb of Babalon, the None itself. If mothering lullabies to their children to lull them to sleep, the Perfection of Understanding sings this mantra of great magick that they may awake. This mantra is not directed at any goal or at any god, it is directed at the true nature of None itself; it *is* the true nature of None itself if it is understood.

The mantra itself has no meaning, for meaning belongs to the realm of knowledge, not Understanding. The meaning cannot be explained: it is incommunicable, as is all real Truth. The mantra is not there to be deciphered by the intellect, it is there to be silently repeated. The Master practices the deep practice, she does not talk about it or describe its meaning. Woe unto me for attempting such a misguided feat!

Nonetheless, if we were to look into the meaning of the mantra, for the sake of the hungry mind, we can find one, keeping in mind that the meaning is not itself the Perfection of Understanding.

The original text has the first word of the mantra as "*gate*," which means "gone" and comes from the root that means "understood." It is thus a direct translation in a way, and because it means "understood," we can see that it refers to the nature of the Perfection of Understanding itself. The term "gone" means someone who has gone or crossed to the other shore from that of Two to that of None. It also refers to the fact that a Master of the Temple is "gone," there is no one left after draining out every last drop of separation, of ego, of self. One can never attain the grade of becoming a Master because there is then no one there who can attain or fail to attain. As it says in our Holy Books, "Yet shalt thou not be therein, for thou shalt be forgotten, dust lost in dust."[35] Further, "gone" is formed of the two consonants "GN." This "GN" forms the root of both "gnosis" and "generation." As the Master has said, "the root GN signifies both knowledge and generation combined in a single idea, in an absolute form independent of personality."[355] It is "knowledge" in the sense that it refers to *gnosis,* which is simply another name for transcendent knowledge, the Perfection of Understanding itself. It is "generation" because it is identical with the ultimate Creative Force, that which creates and destroys yet is untouched by either. This is why it is called *pangenetor,* all-begetter, and *panphage,* all-destroyer, even as None creates, sustains, destroys, and ultimately transcends All. It passes from generation to generation unscathed and unchanged because its nature is beyond space, time, and causality though revealed therein. It is "independent of personality" because the Master has destroyed the personal in the Impersonal, being divested of all duality in the ultimate Naught beyond even the duality of None and Two. All of these ideas are simultaneously present in the word "gone."

In the original text, the next word is *paragate,* which means "into the gone beyond" or "into the understanding beyond." The next word after that is *parasamgate,* which means "in the gone completely beyond" or "into the understanding completely beyond." The Master is gone beyond all things, having crossed the Abyss into the "beyond" of the Supernal Triad, the Womb of Understanding, the None. It is completely beyond all categories, completely beyond all language, completely beyond all things. Thus the mantra continues, "gone beyond, gone completely beyond."

The mantra in the original text concludes with *bodhi svaha.* The first word, *bodhi,* means "enlightenment" and the second word, *svaha,* is an exclamation like "amen" or "hallelujah." In place of *bodhi,* we have the word "hriliu," which comes from *The Vision and the Voice* and is essentially the sound of orgasm. This is used because it refers to the nature of enlightenment itself, formless and timeless ecstasy. It has a further sexual connotation implying the complete union and consummation of two things in ecstasy, which is simply a metaphor for subject and object uniting in *samadhi* wherein Naught remains (in both senses of the word).

The term "ha" replaces that of *svaha* that occurs in the original text. This "ha" is identical with the "Ha!" that is said towards the beginning of this sutra, and it has the same meaning. *Svaha* is an exclamation similar to "hallelujah" and so is "ha." Ha is a way to express ecstasy that is found in and an expression of enlightenment, of *bodhi,* of "hriliu." It has the connotation of a laugh, and it is exclaimed with, as the Master has said, "the confident smile of the immortal Child."[356] "Ha" is also the final word of *The Book of the Law,* our holiest Book, and it therefore refers to a sealing or consecration of all that came before. It is an "end" insofar as there is an end to all separateness and therefore to all shadows. Qabalistically, it is composed of the letter Heh and Aleph. Heh refers to the Breath of Life that brings the None into the realm of manifestation, into Two. Aleph refers to the return of the Two to the None, even as it is attributed to the Tarot trump designated as "0." Therefore, even Qabalistically, it refers to the absorption in the Womb of the Infinite, the Perfection of Understanding, the dissolution of all shadows to reveal the unblemished, unbound, and undivided None.

The meanings of this mantra of great magick are many, but they all refer to the None. The syllables of this mantra of great magick are many, but they are all None. The mantra works no magick at all through being analyzed, described, and explained; it works only through being worked, it does only through being done. Through this doing we may be undone to become None, to be gone, gone, gone beyond, gone completely beyond, hriliu ha.

"If you see your nature, you do not need to read *sutras* or invoke *buddhas*. Erudition and knowledge are not only useless but also cloud your awareness. Doctrines are only for pointing to the mind. Once you see your mind, why pay attention to doctrines? If you do not see your nature, quoting *sutras* is no help."

–Bodhidharma

"Woops!"

–IAO131

1 *Liber LXI vel Causae,* line 5.

2 *Liber Porta Lucis sub figura X,* line 19.

3 This is based on the Brihadaranyaka Upanishad, sometimes translated as "The Book of the Great Forest."

4 The term "play" is a reference to the Hindu term *lila,* which refers to the world being the outcome of the "play" of Brahman, the undifferentiated and limitless Absolute, which is here equated with Horus as the True Self, the Atman that is one with Brahman.

5 "Limitless Light" is a reference to "Ain Soph Aur," one of the Negative Veils on the Qabalistic Tree of Life. "Pure Joy" is a reference to *Liber AL,* II:9, "Existence is pure joy." "True Wisdom and Perfect Happiness" is a reference to the Gnostic Mass.

6 See *The Vision and the Voice,* especially the 12th Aethyr, as well as the Holy Book called *Liber Cheth* for this doctrine of Babalon and her Cup that holds the blood of the saints. Your blood represents "personal life" and the blood in the cup represents "Impersonal Life" - it is therefore that Life that transcends life and death, the Force or Substance that gives rise to all forces and all substances.

7 This is no different whatsoever from the Qabalistic doctrine that the Trinity of Jechidah-Chiah-Neshamah abides eternally in the Supernal Triangle, not limited by the mind (Ruach) or body (Nephesh). In terms of Thelema, this mind and body is the "Khu" that obscures the "Khabs" in one sense and, in another sense, is its necessary means of self-knowledge or manifestation.

8 "Continuity of existence" is a reference to *Liber AL,* I:26, "And the sign shall be my ecstasy, the consciousness of the continuity of existence, the omnipresence of my body."

9 This is a reference to *Liber AL,* I:22, "Now, therefore, I am known to ye by my name Nuit, and to him by a secret name which I will give him when at last he knoweth me. Since I am Infinite Space, and the Infinite Stars thereof, do ye also thus. Bind nothing! Let there be no difference made among you between any one thing & any other thing; for thereby there cometh hurt."

10 "It is not known if it is known" is a direct quotation of *Liber Cheth,* line 21.

11 "Those who are Knowing" refers to those who have achieved *gnosis,* the direct experiential knowledge of Truth or Reality. It is the *jnana* or *gnana* of Yoga.

12 Consider the similarity of this state of consciousness to the Eucharist

of One Element, mentioned in the 20th chapter of *Magick in Theory and Practice*.

13 "Deathless" is, in Greek, *athanatos*, a title applied to the ineffable Lord in the Gnostic Mass. To be "deathless" is to be "imperishable," beyond dissolution or perishing, which only occurs to component, finite phenomena. These component phenomena constitute *samsara*, and the Wheel of Samsara is depicted in Atu X: Fortune; we may therefore visualize Horus as the axle of this Wheel, just as Hadit proclaims of himself in the 2nd chapter of *Liber AL vel Legis*.

14 *Samadhi, kensho, nirvana*, and many another name for the same nameless, non-dual state.

15 Killing out fear is a common goal, yet hope is simply the other side of the coin of fear. This is the mystery spoken of in *Liber LXV*, V:35, "They beheld not God; they beheld not the Image of God; therefore were they arisen to the Palace of the Splendour Ineffable. A sharp sword smote out before them, and the worm Hope writhed in its death-agony under their feet."

16 "Unitive State" is a reference to *samadhi*, the unitive goal of Yoga. The analogy to a man in the arms of his beloved relates the union of subject and object in *samadhi* to the union of male and female in sexual union; this same parallel can be seen in the Gnostic Mass.

17 A desire that requires to be fulfilled implies something unfulfilled, yet the pure will is "unassuaged of purpose," with every action or "desire" being out of an expression of its true Nature, not as an expression of assuaging a lack of fulfillment. Sorrow (*dukkha*) is the result of realizing oneself in a state of not being fulfilled, and one is therefore beyond sorrow insofar as one works with this pure will.

18 "One is alone" is a reference to *Liber AL*, II:23, "I am alone: there is no God where I am."

19 While duality is, in this sense, "wrong" or "evil" insofar as one is obscured from the Truth of Unity, Thelemites only see this as a relative or practical sense of "wrong." Duality is not absolutely evil or wrong in any way; in fact, it is the Limitless Godhead Herself that divides herself for the chance of union, as is proclaimed in the 1st chapter of *Liber AL vel Legis*.

20 A reference to the Gnostic Mass, "May you accomplish your True Wills, the Great Work, the Summum Bonum..."

21 A reference to *Liber AL*, I:31, "They feel little; what is, is balanced by weak joys."

22 This is why pantheism, the notion that God is in all, is but a partial truth. A pantheist believes that everything is God and therefore they are a *part* of God. While this is true on a certain level, we assert that the True Self – the self not identified with body, mind, or any component phenomenon – is actually one with, identical with that True Self. We therefore say that we are not merely part of God but the Ultimate God Itself, a kind of auto-monotheism. Since every man and every woman is a star, each person is this Ultimate God, a kind of poly-monotheism. In this way, one might describe the metaphysic of Thelema as monopolypantheism, which simply goes to show that the traditional divisions of Western metaphysics do not apply well to the initiated understanding of Truth in the Thelemic tradition.

23 The "fool's knots" are a reference to *The Book of Lies,* chapter 61, where Crowley writes "The 'fool' is the Fool of the Tarot, whose number is 0, but refers the the letter Aleph, 1. A fool's knot is a kind of knot which, although it has the appearance of a knot, is not really a knot, but pulls out immediately." The knot therefore refers to duality, separateness, or multiplicity and pulling out the knot refers to entering into identity with the non-dual Self in the Unitive State. "Even now and here" comes from the Thelemic version of the Lord's Prayer that appears in the 2nd chapter of *The Book of Lies.*

24 "Peace" is capitalized to distinguish it from peace that is complementary or opposed to disturbance or war. This Peace is a word for that transcendent state, even as the term *ananda* refers to the Joy that transcends the normal dichotomy of joy and sorrow. Since words are dualistic, and since we are talking about things that are beyond duality, the use of words can be confusing albeit a necessary means of communication.

25 This Self that is seen in others and that others see in oneself is therefore, by definition, not limited to one's personality or ego, that which distinguishes you from others. This Self is a Unity that is expressed in the diversity of selves; it is identical in essence and diverse in expression. This is the foundation of ignorance (*avidya*) that creates the notion of a separate self for the uninitiated, but for the Adept, this is the foundation of the appreciation of the expression of Unity in Diversity.

26 This is based on the Tejobindu Upanishad, sometimes translated as "The Book of the Drop of Divine Splendor."

27 "Knowledge and Conversation" refers to "Knowledge and

Conversation of the Holy Guardian Angel," a term that Crowley adopted from Abramelin for the reason that it is patently absurd (c.f. *Temple of Solomon the King*). People stuck in the intellect will no doubt argue along Qabalistic lines that Knowledge and Conversation is attributed to Tiphareth, a Sephirah on the Tree of Life that is still below the Abyss (i.e. in duality), and therefore this realization is properly attributed to crossing the Abyss in Binah. To this I reply: Sure. Knowledge and Conversation is a term used here to imply that the goal of Thelemic mysticism is nothing other than the same goal of Hindu mysticism, as well as Christian, Muslim, Buddhist, and secular mysticism. To the Adept, these are simply names to choose from at will.

28 One can conveniently attribute these things to the Four Elements, the transcendence of which leads one to identify with the Quintessence, the Fifth Element of Spirit or Aethyr. "The senses" are Earth, "emotional fluctuations" are Water, "likes and dislikes" are Air, and the various identifications of the self are Fire.

29 Horus is Himself a symbol of the union of opposites, of love under will, insofar as he is Two-in-One as Heru-Ra-Ha – containing both active and passive, Ra-Hoor-Khuit and Hoor-paar-kraat, within Himself – as well as by the fact that he is the Child, the union of Father and Mother, containing yet transcending both, c.f. the 1st Aethyr of *The Vision and the Voice.*

30 Consider this in the light of *Liber AL,* II:9, "Existence is pure joy. The sorrows are but as shadows, they pass and are done, but there is that which remains."

31 The piercing and rending of the Veil by the Priest in the Gnostic Mass takes on an extra, mystical dimension with this understanding. The Lance is his Wisdom – his *gnosis* or *jnana* – and the Veil is that which separates him from the Transcendent Light of the Supernal Triad, One-in-Three and Three-in-One, the Holy of Holies, *et cetera ad infinitum.*

32 This is based on the Kena Upanishad, sometimes translated as "The Book of By Whom?"

33 *Liber Cheth vel Vallum Abiegni,* line 21.

34 Baphomet, the Lion-Serpent, is invoked in the Gnostic Mass by the words, "O Lion and O Serpent that destroy the destroyer, be mighty among us!"

35 The invocation of Ra-Hoor-Khuit or Horus in the Gnostic Mass is

accomplished with these words: "Thou that art One, our Lord in the Universe, the Sun, our Lord in ourselves whose name is Mystery of Mystery, uttermost being whose radiance, enlightening the worlds, is also the breath that maketh every God even and Death to tremble before Thee..."

36 These three "Powers" are the three symbols that appear on the rim of the Wheel of Fortune in Atu X of the Tarot. They represent the three gunas: *rajas, tamas,* and *sattvas,* or motion, rest, and balance. Together, they compose the entire universe of which we are aware.

37 "As above, so below" comes from the Emerald Tablet of Hermes. It is the basis of much of Hermeticism that sees a parallel and connection between the Microcosm of Man and the Macrocosm of the Heavens. The Great Work is the unite Microcosm and Macrocosm, Earth and Heaven. Then one knows that one's True Self is actually the Supreme and Ineffable Self, the Self that expresses itself in the Sun, the Lord of the Macrocosm, and in Man, the Lord of the Microcosm.

38 A reference to *Liber AL,* II:6, "I am the flame that burns in every heart of man, and in the core of every star."

39 The reference is to *Liber Librae sub figura XXX,* line 10, "Therefore let thy mental Equilibrium be above disturbance by material events; strengthen and control the animal passions, discipline the emotions and the reason, nourish the Higher Aspirations" and lines 16-17, "To obtain Magical Power, learn to control thought; admit only those ideas that are in harmony with the end desired, and not every stray and contradictory Idea that presents itself. Fixed thought is a means to an end. Therefore pay attention to the power of silent thought and meditation. The material act is but the outward expression of thy thought, and therefore hath it been said that 'the thought of foolishness is sin.' Thought is the commencement of action, and if a chance thought can produce much effect, what cannot fixed thought do?"

40 This is based on the Atma Upanishad, sometimes translated as "The Book of the Supreme Self."

41 This is based on the 5 *yamas* and 5 *niyamas* enumerated by Patanjali in his *Yogasutras.*

42 "Control" is *yama,* and "Virtue" is *niyama.*

43 These five *yamas* of Control come from Patanjali. They are *ahimsa* (non-violence), *satya* (absence of falsehood), *asteya* (non-stealing),

brahmacharya (chastity), and *aparigraha* (non-avarice).

44 These five *niyamas* of Virtue come from Patanjali. They are *shaucha* (cleanliness), *santosha* (contentment), *tapas* (spiritual austerities), *svadhyaya* (study), and *ishvarapranidhana* (surrender to the Lord).

45 In his commentaries on the Holy Book *Liber LXV*, Crowley wrote, "Having attained the Knowledge and Conversation of the Holy Guardian Angel (by a male effort so to speak) the Adept become receptive, feminine, patient, surrendering his will wholly to that of his Angel... The Ego realizes that the Holy Guardian Angel will annihilate it. It trembles, and this shaking of its identity is the token of its surrender... The absolute surrender of the false self is the first condition of the existence of the True Self."

46 In *Liber ABA*, Part II, chapter 6 "The Wand," Crowley writes, "The Magical Will is in its essence twofold, for it presupposes a beginning and an end; to will to be a thing is to admit that you are not that thing. Hence to will anything but the supreme thing, is to wander still further from it – any will but that to give up the self to the Beloved is Black Magick – yet this surrender is so simple an act that to our complex minds it is the most difficult of all acts; and hence training is necessary. Further, the Self surrendered must not be less than the All-Self; one must not come before the altar of the Most High with an impure or an imperfect offering. As it is written in *Liber LXV*, 'To await Thee is the end, not the beginning' ...It is therefore necessary to develop the will to its highest point, even though the last task but one is the total surrender of this will. Partial surrender of an imperfect will is of no account in Magick."

47 This is based on the Isha Upanishad, sometimes translated as "The Book of the Inner Ruler."

48 Similar to the Gnostic Mass, "Thou that art One, our Lord in the Universe the Sun, our Lord in ourselves whose name is Mystery of Mystery..."

49 The Tree of Life is thus the anatomy of Ra-Hoor-Khuit, which is said of him by the Master Therion in *Liber Aleph* and is the basis for Frater Achad's book title *The Anatomy of the Body of God*.

50 In the Anthem of the Gnostic Mass, the Priest invokes, "Thou who art I beyond all I am / who hast no nature and no name / who art when all but Thou are gone; / Thou, centre and secret of the Sun." The Qabalistic image invoked is that of Kether being the point hidden in the center of Tiphareth, the Sun.

51 This is based on the Katha Upanishad, sometimes translated as "The Book of Death as Teacher."

52 Ta-Nech is the father of Ankh-af-na-khonsu. His name occurs in *Liber AL,* III:38, where it is written, "By wise Ta-Nech I weave my spell." His name also occurs in "Across the Gulf" where he is called "the holy and mighty one."

53 Ankh-af-na-khonsu was a priest of Mentu in the 8th century BCE. He is the author of the Stele of Revealing and The Beast 666 identified with him as the Priest of the Princes.

54 This does not mean they will "meet" those who have died in some kind of supra-mundane heaven or hell. It simply means that they too will die like all the others.

55 The West is the place of the setting Sun and therefore the place of death.

56 This Heaven is on Earth. There is not a separate "Heaven" divorced from Earth, but there is a certain consciousness of bliss that is achieved on Earth while living that is called, for convenience, "Heaven."

57 In the Creed of the Gnostic Mass, we say, "And I confess my life one, individual, and eternal that was, and is, and is to come."

58 In *Magick in Theory & Practice,* chapter 18, Crowley writes, "The Magician becomes identical with the immortal Osiris, yet the Magician dies. In this dilemma the facts must be restated. One should preferably say that the Magician becomes conscious of that part of himself which he calls the immortal Osiris; and that Part does not 'die.'"

59 In the 22nd Aethyr of *The Vision and the Voice,* Crowley writes, "In the New Aeon, Death is become Life Triumphant, not through Resurrection, but in its own Essence. The Thelemite does not 'suffer death.' He is eternal and perceives Himself the Universe, by virtue of the categories of Life and Death, which are not real but subjective forms of his artistic presentation."

60 *Liber AL,* II:6, "I am the flame that burns in every heart of man, and in the core of every star. I am Life, and the giver of Life, yet therefore is the knowledge of me the knowledge of death."

61 *Liber AL,* I:61, "For one kiss wilt thou then be willing to give all; but whoso gives one particle of dust shall lose all in that hour."

62 In Thelema, our term Love – Agape – means Union. In the Hindu system, the term Yoga means Union.

63 *Liber AL,* II:7, "I am the Magician and the Exorcist. I am the axle of the wheel, and the cube in the circle. 'Come unto me' is a foolish word: for it is I that go."

64 *Liber AL,* II:9, "Remember all ye that existence is pure joy; that all the sorrows are but as shadows; they pass & are done; but there is that which remains."

65 In the Gnostic Mass, the Priest says thrice, "O Lion and O Serpent that destroy the destroyer, be mighty among us."

66 In the Collect of "The Lord" in the Gnostic Mass, the Deacon intones, "Lord secret and most holy, source of light, source of life, source of love, source of liberty, be thou ever constant and mighty within us, force of energy, fire of motion; with diligence let us ever labour with thee, that we may remain in thine abundant joy."

67 Qabalistically, this is the Sphere of Malkuth, the *nephesh.*

68 On his second step toward the Veil, the Priest says, "O secret of secrets that art hidden in the being of all that lives, not Thee do we adore, for that which adoreth is also Thou. Thou art That, and That am I."

69 This "super-conscious way of knowing" is the *neschamah,* attributed to Binah above the Abyss, in contrast to the *ruach,* the conscious and rational mind, which is below the Abyss, centered in Tiphareth.

70 The original text has the phrases, "Get up! Wake up!" The reference here is to *Liber AL,* II:34, "But ye, o my people, rise up & awake!"

71 This is why the Lord is "secret and ineffable" and why Crowley says in *Magick in Theory & Practice,* chapter 9, that "all real secrets are incommunicable."

72 Direct and experiential knowledge is *gnosis* as opposed to normal, rational knowledge. It pertains to *neschamah* rather than the *ruach.*

73 "Wisdom" is the 2ⁿᵈ Sephirah of Chokmah, "Understanding" is the 3ʳᵈ Sephirah of Binah, and "Beauty" is the 6ᵗʰ Sephirah of Tiphareth. Together, they form the descending triangle that is a symbol of Ra-Hoor-Khuit, the Lord of Love.

74 This parallels the first lines of the Bible as in Genesis 1:2, "And the earth was without form, and void; and darkness was upon the face of the deep. And the Spirit of God moved upon the face of the waters..."

75 In the Anthem of the Gnostic Mass, the Priest gives an invocation that is essentially identical with the message regarding the Supreme Self in this chapter: "Thou who art I, beyond all I am, / Who hast no

nature and no name, / Who art, when all but thou are gone, / Thou, centre and secret of the Sun, / Thou, hidden spring of all things known / And unknown, Thou aloof, alone, / Thou, the true fire within the reed / Brooding and breeding, source and seed / Of life, love, liberty, and light, / Thou beyond speech and beyond sight, / Thee I invoke, my faint fresh fire / Kindling as mine intents aspire. / Thee I invoke, abiding one, / Thee, centre and secret of the Sun, / And that most holy mystery / Of which the vehicle am I. / Appear, most awful and most mild, / As it is lawful, in thy child!"

76 *Liber AL,* II:2-3, "Come! all ye, and learn the secret that hath not yet been revealed. I, Hadit, am the complement of Nu, my bride. I am not extended, and Khabs is the name of my House. 3. In the sphere I am everywhere the centre, as she, the circumference, is nowhere found."

77 *Liber AL,* I:51, "There are four gates to one palace; the floor of that palace is of silver and gold; lapis lazuli & jasper are there; and all rare scents; jasmine & rose, and the emblems of death. Let him enter in turn or at once the four gates; let him stand on the floor of the palace..."

78 This is the Wheel of Fortune, the Wheel of Jupiter seen in Atu X: Fortune.

79 This is a reference to the Collect of "Earth" in the Gnostic Mass: "Mother of fertility on whose breast lieth water, whose cheek is caressed by air, and in whose heart is the sun's fire, womb of all life, recurring grace of seasons..."

80 These are the traditional "elementals" of the four classical Elements.

81 The "breath of life" is related to the letter "A" of AUMGN as the sound of Birth, and it is also related to the letters "GN" of AUMGN as the breath of life as opposed to that of speech, i.e. the impersonal and deathless Life as opposed to the dualistic and temporal life.

82 As it is said in *Liber AL,* II:9, "Remember all ye that existence is pure joy; that all the sorrows are but as shadows; they pass & are done; but there is that which remains."

83 The ineffable, invisible, intangible Self is the Supreme Self, and it is reflected into the Heavens and Earth as the "visible and sensible" Sun and every Man/Woman (respectively).

84 Horus encompasses the entire cosmos, and therefore, in Qabalistic language, the Tree of Life is a map of his "anatomy."

85 This passage from *Liber LXV,* II:4-6, similarly describes the descent

of the Godhead or Divine Consciousness into the duality of matter: "Stooping down, dipping my wings, I came unto the darkly-splendid abodes. There in that formless abyss was I made a partaker of the Mysteries Averse. I suffered the deadly embrace of the Snake and of the Goat; I paid the infernal homage to the shame of Khem. Therein was this virtue, that the One became the all."

86 *Liber Porta Lucis,* line 20, "The many change and pass; the one remains."

87 This image of the Tree of Life with the root in Kether and its branches or fruit in Malkuth is seen in the alchemical text *Philosophia Sacra* (1626) by Robert Fludd.

88 This is based on the Mandukya Upanishad, sometimes translated as "The Book of the Medium of Awareness."

89 Liber Librae, line 18, "Therefore, as hath already been said, Establish thyself firmly in the equilibrium of forces, in the centre of the Cross of the Elements, that Cross from whose centre the Creative Word issued in the birth of the Dawning Universe."

90 The Creed of the Gnostic Mass states, "I confess my life one, individual, and eternal that was, and is, and is to come."

91 Qabalistically, the Silence is 0, the Negative Veils of Existence that are pre-existent, so to speak, to Kether and the rest of the Tree of Life. Since it is beyond duality, it is beyond the categories of duality: space, time, and causality.

92 Countenance not beholding countenance refers to an old Qabalistic adage, "Before there was equilibrium, countenance beheld not countenance." Beauty not beholding beauty refers to the Marriage Collect of the Gnostic Mass, "...may strength and skill unite to bring forth ecstasy, and beauty answer beauty." Because this is before duality, countenance does not behold countenance and beauty does not answer beauty.

93 As it says in *Liber AL,* I:22, "Bind nothing! Let there be no difference made among you between any one thing & any other thing; for thereby there cometh hurt."

94 This Bodhi-Tree is the Tree of Life itself and is analogous to the Mahalingam of Shiva as well as Yggdrasil, the "world-ash wonder-tree" mentioned in the Gnostic Mass. It is the *axis mundi* or cosmic axis found in virtually every culture's mythology.

95 This is Atu 0: The Fool, and the babe is Harpocrates or Hoor-paar-kraat, the Lord of Silence. They are forms or names of Horus, the

Crowned and Conquering Child.

96 Speech implies vibration, which represents duality. Silence therefore represents non-duality. For there to be "Speech in the Silence" implies the outburst of duality from non-duality, the 0 expressing itself in complementary opposites of 1 and -1 (or X and -X).

97 This Word is the Word of God, the Logos. It is spoken of in John 1:1-5, "In the beginning was the Word, and the Word was with God, and the Word was God. The same was in the beginning with God. All things were made by him; and without him was not any thing made that was made. In him was life; and the life was the light of men. And the light shineth in darkness; and the darkness comprehended it not."

98 The letter "A" is the first letter of the alphabet and its cognate letter is the first in most alphabets (Alpha in Greek, Aleph in Hebrew, Alif in Arabic, *et cetera*). Insofar as it is the first, it represents the Beginning or Birth.

99 Anything that is created will be destroyed, anything that is born will die, anything that arises will fall. That is the law of the world of *maya* or *samsara,* yet it is only thereby that experience is possible.

100 This is literally seen in every Gnostic Mass and is seen to reflect the same idea that all which is born must die.

101 This is both joyful and sorrowful. The line is a reference to *Liber Cheth,* lines 17-18, "And this is the wrath of God, that these things should be thus. And this is the grace of God, that these things should be thus."

102 In the language of Christianity, this is the Fall of Man which makes possible its Redemption through Grace, which is merely a restatement of 1 Corinthians 15:22, "For as in Adam all die, even so in Christ shall all be made alive." In this light, the Word of AUMGN is identified with the Word or Logos of Christ as both creator of duality (as in John 1:1-5) and the redeemer therefrom. In the language of Eastern philosophies, this is the ignorance of man (duality) which makes possible its illumination through wisdom or illumination (union).

103 This is the Vav of Hebrew, which is attributed to Taurus and Atu V: The Hierophant. Taurus is the Bull, a symbol of discipline and directed force.

104 This shows the U of AUM as the Sun at noon, i.e. at its brightest. In this way, A is seen as sunrise/birth, U as noon/life, and M as

sunset/death. Also, the Master has said, "U or V is the manifested son himself. Its number is 6. It refers therefore, to the dual nature of the Logos as divine and human; the interlacing of the upright and averse triangles in the hexagram. It is the first number of the Sun, whose last number is 666, 'the number of a man.'" The phrase "far-darting rays" is a reference to the Chaldean Oracles.

105 U corresponds to Vav to which is attributed Atu V: The Hierophant. On older versions of this card, the Hierophant carries a staff topped by the "Elevenfold cross" that symbolizes the entire Tree of Life. In Atu V, the symbols of the Four Elemenets are in the corners, showing the balance of the Four Elements and the Four Powers of the Sphinx.

106 A reference to the Collect of the Sun in the Gnostic Mass.

107 A reference to the Collect of Marriage in the Gnostic Mass.

108 Beauty is the literal meaning of "Tiphareth," the 6th Sephirah of the Tree of Life that corresponds to the Sun and ideas such as balance and centrality. The reference is, in general, to seeing Unity-in-Diversity.

109 M is the Hebrew letter Mem to which is attributed the Element of Water. M is also the letter of "mater," mother, and "mort," death.

110 This letter is attributed to the setting Sun. The god Tum is attributed to this quarter of the day and his name likewise ends in the "M" sound.

111 During the Collect of Death in the Gnostic Mass, everyone stands upright, head erect, eyes open. This shows everyone standing firm, open, and courageous in the face of death, which is the basic attitude in the New Aeon toward death.

112 This is the Uraeus serpent on the Priest's crown that makes him a Priest of the Lord. "Mighty, Woundless, Deathless" are appellations of the Lord used in the invocation of the rending of the Veil in the Gnostic Mass, i.e. *ischuron, athanaton, abroton.*

113 From the Collect of the Saints from the Gnostic Mass: "Lord of Life and Joy, that art the might of man, that art the essence of every true god that is upon the surface of the earth, continuing knowledge from generation unto generation."

114 The reference is to *samadhi,* the union of subject and object in meditation. It has been analyzed as *sam,* "together with," *adhi,* "the Lord," and therefore refers to union with one's True Self, the Lord Horus.

115 "Procreative life-will" is a phrase that Nietzsche uses in *Thus Spoke Zarathustra* to describe the Will-to-Power, which he sees as the fundamental nature of all things.

116 Pan, or "All," is called *panphage*, "all-destroyer," and *pangenetor*, "all-begetter," i.e. creator and destroyer.

117 The reference is to Hadit, the axle of the wheel, c.f. *Liber AL*, chapter 2.

118 This is Khephra, the god of the Sun attributed to the quarter of midnight, who bears the Sun-disk in his mandibles. It refers in general to rebirth.

119 "Certain, and most true" is a reference to the Emerald Tablet of Hermes, which begins with the line, "This is true without lie, certain and most true." I have always found it a little disconcerting for anyone to begin by asserting the truth of what they are going to say before it's even said. Don't you think?

120 "Many another un-words" is an obscure reference to the list of Saints in the Gnostic Mass where a couple lists of names with the phrase "and many another..." There is a virtue to expendiency in ritual.

121 "Laughterful caresses" is a reference to *Liber AL*, II:63, "Thou art exhaust in the voluptuous fullness of the inspiration; the expiration is sweeter than death, more rapid and laughterful than a caress of Hell's own worm."

122 Søren Kierkegaard (1813-1855) was an existential philosopher who basically formulated the idea we know of as the "leap of faith" where one's knowledge has gaps and one can think and argue and debate and be skeptical, yet at a certain point one must make a leap and believe or at least start acting without thinking too much. This, obviously, has positive and negative aspects but the whole point is that even an omniscient narrator has to make a leap of faith at a certain point. Does *everything* need to be spelled out for you?

123 Jonah was, of course, the Pinnochio of his day, having been swallowed by a great sea creature in a story that comes from a certain collection of poorly-written fables. Being the anti-Jonah therefore implies a willing (rather than involuntary) engulfment in the great sea creature's belly.

124 Harpocrates is a Greek form of the Egyptian Horus, and he was the god of Silence. He is used in ceremonial magick to represent silence, defense, and the unmanifest potential of Existence.

125 The Great Womb of Time is a reference to the Qabalistic sphere of Binah, the Great Mother of form, whose color is black and to whom is attributed Saturn, Chronos, Kali, *et cetera.*

126 The Path of Return refers to a certain system of enlightenment where the original Fall from Eden, or the Supernal Triangle, is rectified by returning thereto.

127 The ram's horn is the Jewish shofar which is blown to mark important times of the year. The use of the shofar is here conflated with – er, I mean 'skillfully synthesized with' – the uttering of the true pronunciation of the Tetragrammaton by the High Priest of the Temple.

128 The reference is to *Liber AL,* III:34, "...another soul of God and beast shall mingle in the globed priest..."

129 "Out of the mouth of babes" is a phrase that originally comes from the New Testament, and it has come to refer to Tom Hanks in the movie "Big." It otherwise refers to the fact that children often speak surprising truths.

130 "God is dead" as Nietzsche said, "and we have killed him." You've been caught red-handed, dear reader, but I won't tell anyone.

131 The Five Precepts are an ethical code taken by the laypeople of Theravada and some forms of Mahayana Buddhism, which include (1) abstaining from taking life, (2) abstaining from stealing, (3) abstaining from sexual misconduct, (4) abstaining from false speech, and (5) abstaining from alcohol and other intoxicants. Those who understand the truth of *anatta* simultaneously perceive these Five Precepts as an incredibly bad joke by the Buddha.

132 Crossing the "Rubicon" means that one has reached the point of no return and is a reference to Caesar's crossing of the river, which started a civil war. It is an obscure way to refer to the war on oneself that occurs both in starting puberty and becoming an ascetic.

133 The Three Characteristics are *dukkha* (suffering), *anicca* (impermanence), and *anatta* (no-self). The Three Refuges are in *buddha* (the awakened one), *dharma* (the teaching of the Buddha), and *sangha* (the monastic community). The Four Noble truths are (1) the diagnosis of *dukkha,* (2) its etiology, (3) its prognosis, and (4) its treatment. The Five Precepts are explained above, and I'm too lazy to repeat myself.

134 The Two Truths doctrine refers to the differentiation between relative or conventional truth on the one hand and absolute or

ultimate truth on the other hand. The Three Characteristics, Three Refuges, Four Noble Truths, and Five Precepts are explained above. The Five Aggregates refer to the ever-changing clusters of form, sensation, perception, mental formations, and consciousness itself that create the illusion of solidity of self and world. The Six Senses refer to the five normal senses and the mind as the sixth sense. The Seven Factors of Enlightenment refer to seven factors or virtues that lead to enlightenment including mindfulness, discernment, energy, joy, tranquility, concentration, and equanimity. The Eightfold Path refers to the eight non-sequential steps that Buddha gave as the treatment for the ailment of suffering. The Nine Yanas refer to nine spiritual practices as delineated by a school of Tibetan Buddhism. The Ten Perfections are ten qualities or paramitas of awakened ones. The Twelve Links or *nidanas* of Dependent Origination refer to the twelve interdependent causes of *samsara*. The Fourteen Unanswerable Questions refer to fourteen questions about metaphysics that the Buddha refused to answer.

135 Harold putting his sandals on his head refers to the 14th koan in The Gateless Gate where Nansen comes upon monks arguing over a cat, cuts the cat in two pieces, and Joshu, upon hearing this from Nansen, places his sandals on his head and walked out of the room whereupon Nansen said, "If you had been there, you could have saved the cat."

136 The Grade of $2°=9^\square$ refers to the "Zelator" grade of A∴A∴, which is a system of spiritual advancement in the Western Esoteric Tradition. Since 2 refers to the 2nd Sephirah of Chokmah on the Tree of Life, to which is attributed Force and Change, and 9 refers to the 9th Sephirah of Yesod, to which is attributed the Foundation and Stability, the equation of 2 and 9 refers to the resolution of the paradox of Motion and Rest.

137 The knocking of 3, then 5, then 3 refers to the series of knocks that is used in "saying Will" in Thelema and in other rituals. It adds to a total of 11 knocks, the number of the Great Work accomplished, where the 5, or Microcosm, is in the midst of or united with the 6, or Macrocosm.

138 Harold asking about meddling with the Goetia refers to Allan Bennett (a.k.a. Bhikku Ananda Metteya) saying something similar to Aleister Crowley upon meeting him.

139 "The car called Millions-of-Years" is a reference to a line from

Liber LXV, a Holy Book of Thelema. It is itself likely a reference to the Sun being conceived as a 'car' or 'bark' or boat that sails across the firmament. In any case, Harold is suffering from a fit of grandiosity.

140 "Loosening the girders of the soul" is a reference to *Liber AL*, III:61, "There is an end of the word of the God enthroned in Ra's seat, lightening the girders of the soul."

141 The dirty dishes being "piled up at random" is a reference to Heraclitus who wrote, "The fairest universe is but a heap of rubbish piled up at random."

142 "What in Geb's name are you blathering about" is a reference to a similar line from *The Big Lebowski*, and Geb is a name of an Egyptian god of earth. He worships a god of Earth, i.e. the friend is a typical secular materialist, lacking any sense of purpose or wonder.

143 "*Panta rhei*" means "everything changes" or "everything flows," which is a saying attributed to Heraclitus, and the general idea being discussed is similar to Heraclitus' notion that one cannot step into the same river twice.

144 "I am not who I am" is a reference to a similar line said by Iago in Othello, which is an inversion of the Biblical "I am that I am" that Jehovah said was his name when speaking from a burning bush in that old, crazy ass book of myths.

145 "Nothing lasts, but nothing is lost" is the name of an album by the band "Shpongle" who made hella trippy music, man. Who knew that *The Big Lebowski*, Egyptian gods, Heraclitus, and *The Bible* could all be strung together in a single piece of conversation?

146 "I have no need of that hypothesis" was said by the physicist LaPlace when supposedly asked by Napoleon where the Creator was in his work on astronomy. Or something. I can't really remember the details, but it seemed like a badass thing to say.

147 "The world is only justifiable as an aesthetic phenomenon" is a reference to a virtually identical line from Friedrich Nietzsche's *The Birth of Tragedy*. Or that's at least my distorted memory of it.

148 "Everything that is, is enough" is something that Osho's mother said to him, or something similar to that – as you can see, I tend to cite and reference things even though I can't really even remember what they are. That isn't very congruent with being an omniscient narrator, is it?

149 The Motley Cow is the name of a town in Thus Spake Zarathustra.

150 The third and fifth precepts refer to abstaining from sexual misconduct and abstaining from imbibing alcohol, respectively. But you're keeping track anyhow, aren't you?

151 The Dweller on the Threshold is a figure in Western occultism that is either seen as the Guardian of the Mysteries or a personification of one's "evil" or shadow side.

152 "Some men are born posthumously" is a reference to a similar saying by Friedrich Nietzsche who used it to refer to himself.

153 "Is there no help for the widow's son" is a reference to the distress call of a Master Mason who has read *The Da Vinci Code*.

154 "Mea culpa, mea culpa, mea maxima culpa" means "my fault, my fault, my most grievous fault," and is said in Catholic liturgy as a form of confessing yourself as a helpless, hopeless, shameful sack of sin.

155 "purse-proud yet ultimately penniless" refers to a line from *Liber LXV*, a Holy Book of Thelema. The entire metaphor of the tavern as a place where Adepts get spiritual intoxication comes from the same section of the same book.

156 It is said that no man hath lifted Her veil because Isis is an incredibly persistent tease.

157 This is a stolen Oscar Wilde quote: "Fashion is a form of ugliness so intolerable that we have to alter it every six months."

158 Mammon represents money. The reference is to Matthew 6:24, "No man can serve two masters: for either he will hate the one, and love the other; or else he will hold to the one, and despise the other. Ye cannot serve God and mammon."

159 The "noble savage" is what is glorified in *Running with Wolves, Fern Gully, Avatar,* and generally all movies that spring from white guilt. Ironic that it is the White man that is always the savages' savior, isn't it?

160 This is stolen from *The Book of Lies,* chapter 79, "Nature is wasteful; but how well She can afford it! Nature is false; but I'm a bit of a liar myself. Nature is useless; but then how beautiful she is! Nature is cruel; but I too am a Sadist."

161 Pascal made a wager, and the jury is still out to whether he lost it or not.

162 Immanuel is Immanuel Kant, the person who found Reason to be the royal road to Truth, and his name ironically means, "God is with us."

163 A typical red herring used by Rabbis to avoid the inevitable conclusion following from their premises.

164 This last bit is from Friedrich Nietzsche's *The Gay Science.*

165 John Keats said, "Truth is beauty, and beauty truth." He is endlessly praised for this tautology, but I find it fairly boring.

166 The Parable of the Sower is a parable told by Christ where he conceals his sex addiction.

167 The general form of using logic to transcend logic is an incredibly poor imitation of Nagarjuna's treatment of different Buddhist concepts through his Middle Path.

168 The opposite of Good being Bad refers to an essay by Nietzsche in his book *The Genealogy of Morals*, where he contrasts the "Good versus Bad" attitude of Masters with the "Good versus Evil" attitude of Slaves.

169 "Punctuality is the thief of time" is a principle of Lord Henry's in Oscar Wilde's *The Picture of Dorian Gray.*

170 Lord Alfred Douglas, or "Bosie," was Wilde's lover. It is actually a reference to Aleister Crowley who wrote, "The Golden Rule is silly. If Lord Alfred Douglas (for example) did to others what he would like them to do to him, many would resent his action."

171 Luckily, the fool that said this chose hemlock to rid us of a nuisance.

172 Philosophy being an unconscious autobiography of its author is an idea that comes from the first chapter of Nietzsche's *Beyond Good & Evil.*

173 "A fool who persists in his folly becomes wise" is a quotation from William Blake.

174 The demonstration is a form of the argument against utilitarianism that a gladiator being slaughtered in a coliseum is ethical because it entertains thousands of people even though the gladiator suffers and dies.

175 The idea of people being polluted streams and the prophet being an ocean comes from Nietzsche's *Thus Spake Zarathustra*. He can be a little condescending at times, I guess.

176 The setting is a reference to an actual cliff-side in Big Sur, California. This chapter is actually a disguised Magical Record.

177 The mention of Bob Dylan is a reference to his song "Blowin' in the Wind." You seriously needed to look that one up?

178 "Om nom nom" is the sound of someone eating and chewing food,

hence the reference to the All-Devourer, or "*Panphage*," which is a title of the god Pan. Internet humor, I guess... sorry about that.

179 The "sexual-electric energy" is a reference to a certain somatic sensation that is common in the first couple hours of taking LSD.

180 "Spartan futility" refers to the movie "300," both in content and quality.

181 The "dreamless sleep" and the "wave-less, reflection-less pond" are references to metaphors used by Patanjali and other Yogis to refer to the state of pure awareness that is achieved upon attaining *samadhi*. It is here equated with the crossing of the Abyss in the language of Thelemic mysticism.

182 Being "cast back out of the Abyss" refers to the idea that the Magister Templi, i.e. one who has successfully extinguished the ego and crossed the Abyss, is cast back into duality. Crowley said that one is cast back into a certain Sephirah to do a certain task relevant to it. For example, Buddha was cast back into the Sphere of Mercury to relate his insights in the language of objective rationality, Rumi was cast back into the Sphere of Venus to convey his attainment through devotional poetry, To Mega Therion was cast back into the Sphere of Jupiter to become a Paternal-Initiator figure or something, et cetera.

183 "A star falling upon the darkness of the earth" is a reference to *Liber LXV*, V:5, as well as the Star of Wormwood from the Book of Revelation in the New Testament, and the "morning star" in general... all of which refer to the Messiah or Savior coming to earth.

184 Khephra is an Egyptian god in the form of a scarab who carries the Sun in its mandibles, often attributed to the Sun at Dawn (or Midnight in the Thelemic solar Adoration of "Liber Resh").

185 The Night of Pan, or "N.O.X.," is a name for the state of non-duality or non-ego after having crossed the Abyss.

186 "Shot like lightning" refers to the Lightning Flash in the Qabalah, which is a symbol of the Divine Unity emanating and manifesting into the ten Sephiroth of the Tree of Life in an instant. The "Limitless Light" is a translation of the Hebrew phrase "Ain Soph Aur," which is a Negative Veil before the the first Sephirah, Kether, on the Tree of Life.

187 "Anatta" is one of the Buddhist Three Characteristics of existence, which means "not-self." The idea is that *anatta* is seen as an enema that clears out Harold who was full of shit, so to speak. Get it?

188 The "Positionless Position" is a reference to the "zero state" achieved in satori as described in Zen Buddhism. It is a good example of the characteristic paradoxicality of the utterances of virtually all mystics. Go read Walter Stace!

189 The stringed instrument is a reference to the story of Buddha coming upon a similar situation after his enlightenment, leading him to create the Middle Way as a string must be neither too lose nor too taught. The "straight and narrow way" is a reference to the path to the Kingdom of Heaven from the New Testament. The tightrope walker is a reference to Nietzsche's Zarathustra who comes upon a similar situation after coming down from his mountain.

190 "Satori" is a name for the non-dual state of awakened perception in Zen Buddhism. Didn't I already mention that like half a page ago? Kids these days...

191 Harold "roaring" the line "the air was burdened and hungry clouds swagged on the deep" are references to the prophet Rintrah in William Blake's *The Marriage of Heaven and Hell.*

192 The various reactions of the crowd to Harold's pronouncement are an obscure reference to Christ's Parable of the Sower. Wikipedia it.

193 "Maya" is the Hindu name for the illusion of the world.

194 "Hibernation sickness" is a reference to *The Return of the Jedi.* What, you knew that one? Nerd.

195 The "Ultimate Naught" is a reference to the Qabalistic Zero, which is not a "lack of something," but a name for the continuous, all-containing Unmanifest.

196 The reference is to *Liber AL,* II:70, "There is help & hope in other spells. Wisdom says: be strong! Then canst thou bear more joy. Be not animal; refine thy rapture! If thou drink, drink by the eight and ninety rules of art: if thou love, exceed by delicacy; and if thou do aught joyous, let there be subtlety therein!"

197 "Is everything alright? I am God, and this farce is my creation" is a virtually direct quotation of Friedrich Nietzsche, who wrote this in a letter during his last years of "insanity."

198 The Dorje and Phurba are "weapons" of Tibetan Buddhism that are equatable to some extent to the Wand and Dagger in Western ceremonial magick and to the fork or skewer and knife in Western cooking.

199 A "Master of the Temple" or "Magister Templi" is someone who has successfully crossed the Abyss and achieved the grade of $8°=3^\square$

in A∴A∴, and he therefore has the authority to formulate a new Outer Order.

200 The Secret Chiefs are the illuminated Adepts or praeter-human intelligences that are said to watch over humanity and send a Magus to bring a Word of Truth every now and then, similar to the Hindu idea that Vishnu will incarnate to bring balance to the Universe every so often.

201 "The Pure Fool" is a reference to the Tarot Trump called "The Fool," which is attributed to the number 0.

202 See "The Perfection of Understanding Sutra" later in this book for more on this idea.

203 These are references to *Liber AL*, II:5, "Behold! the rituals of the old time are black. Let the evil ones be cast away; let the good ones be purged by the prophet! Then shall this Knowledge go aright" and *Liber AL*, I:38, "He must teach; but he may make severe the ordeals."

204 This entire quotation – "Honestly... or where one lives" – is virtually a direct quotation of Friedrich Nietzsche from his "insanity letters" written at the end of his life. It's almost as if he had some illuminated insight and wasn't just insane, huh?

205 "Wonder-Tree Sap" is a reference to the Anthem of "Liber XV: The Gnostic Mass" where the line "sap of the world-ash wonder-tree" occurs. It could be seen as a veiled way to ask for Harold's semen – it *could,* but then you'd be a pervert, of course.

206 The reference is to *Liber AL*, II:58, "Yea! deem not of change: ye shall be as ye are, & not other. Therefore the kings of the earth shall be Kings for ever: the slaves shall serve. There is none that shall be cast down or lifted up: all is ever as it was..."

207 The "Crowned and Conquering Child" is a name of Horus, a symbol of Godhead in Thelema. I hope you have figured that one out already, but I figured I would err on the side of safety.

208 The mention of Elijah and chairs is a reference to the Jewish practice of leaving an empty chair during the ceremony of Passover for Elijah to occupy.

209 "The soul is already perfect: Perfect purity, perfect calm, perfect silence" is an adaptation of a line from Aleister Crowley's essay "The Soul of the Desert."

210 The "Veil of Mother Matter" refers to the Veil of Isis "that no man hath lifted."

211 "I am the Truth" is an utterance of mystics from Jesus Christ to Mansur al-Hallaj. Both were punished with death for such blasphemous indiscretions.

212 A "black brother" is an "evil" or "left-hand path" magician who refuses to dissolve his ego into the Absolute, shutting himself up out of selfishess. It is the mystical equivalent to being anal retentive and therefore full of shit.

213 "Choronzon" is a name given to the "devil" of incoherence and dispersion that abides in the Abyss. Choronzon appears in a well-known chapter of Aleister Crowley's *The Vision and the Voice*, which details his astral explorations of the Enochian Aethyrs.

214 The woman is an archetypal expression of the Terrible Mother, as described by Carl Jung in several of his books. She appears here in the form of Kali.

215 Pyrrho was a famous Ancient Greek skeptic after which the Pyrrhonian school of skepticism was named.

216 The "primitive atlas for the dream world" is an obscure reference to an appendix in Aleister Crowley's *Magick in Theory & Practice* that is entitled "Notes for an Astral Atlas."

217 Chuang Tzu or Zhuangzi was a Taoist sage who was only second in importance to Lao Tzu.

218 A reference to Crowley's *The Wake World*.

219 The chapter title is a reference to Swinburne's poem "Atalanta in Calydon" where the Chorus ends a speech with the lines, "He weaves, and is clothed with derision; / Sows, and he shall not reap; / His life is a watch or a vision / Between a sleep and a sleep."

220 "Malkuth" is the 10th and final Sephirah on the Tree of Life, which refers to the material world. The common metaphor of the Great Work is to climb the Tree of Life from Malkuth back to Kether, the 1st Sephirah of the Tree of Life. The first Path after Malkuth is the Path of Tav, which is attributed to traveling on the astral plane or "scrying in the spirit vision."

221 The various items on the table are symbolic of Harold consecrating the mundane implements as magical weapons. The "Solomonic pillars" refers to the pillars of duality known as "Jachin" and "Boaz" in Freemasonry, which represent Heaven and Earth; similar pillars are seen in various Western esoteric sects and are often black and white to show duality through color. The "three-pronged wand" is a reference to the Hebrew letter Shin, which is symbolic of the "Ruach

Elohim" or "Holy Spirit" and is attributed to the Element of Fire, like the Wand, in occultism.

222 "Apple pancake diamond hoes" is a corruption of "Apo pantos kakodaimonos," which means "Away all evil spirits" and is said at the beginning of the ritual known as "The Star Ruby" as an initial banishing.

223 The "Qliphoth" are the shells that lie beneath Malkuth on the Tree of Life and represent the dark or inverted aspects of the universe. The priest being affected by the banishing is a reference to Aleister Crowley's suggestion in his Eight Lectures on Yoga to say "Apo pantos kakodaimonos" whenever encountering a man of cloth so as to banish evil influences from one's magical Circle, so to speak.

224 The Sign of the Enterer is a grade sign of the Neophyte degree in the Hermetic Order of the Golden Dawn, which referes to the force of Horus/Ra-Hoor-Khuit as opposed to the silence of Hoor-paar-kraat/Harpocrates.

225 "Astral portal" is a reference to the practice in the Golden Dawn of imagining a door or image through which one passes in order to enter the astral plane.

226 "The world was without form and void" is a direction quotation from the beginning of the Old Testament where it refers to the world before Creation.

227 The "Blue Angel" is a reference to the American acrobatic fighter planes with a double-meaning of being a reference to angels who are considered beings that exist on the subtler planes and blue being a color of aspiration or prayer (as in the ascending blue triangle that complements the descending red triangle of Horus in the Hexagram of Magick, c.f. Crowley's *The Book of Lies*, chapter 69).

228 "Pre-regulation, destroyer-class, solid-fuel recoil boosters" is a reference to the 1995 PC game "Full Throttle" where the main character attaches such boosters to his motorcycle in order to jump over an impassable gorge. It was a really cool game.

229 The "deva-world of Tusita" is a reference to one of the Buddhist "heavens" where certain Bodhisattvas abide.

230 "Tathagatagarbha Madhyamaka Avalokitesvara Padmasambhava Prajnaparamita Nirodha-Samapatti" is a name composed of stringing together different Buddhist concepts and names of Bodhisattvas to make fun of the long and over-indulgent titles of supposedly enlightened people. "Tathagatagarbha" means "Thus gone" or

"Thus-crossed one" and refers to the Mahayana doctrine that Buddha-nature is already present and within everyone; "Madhyamaka" is the name of Nagarjuna's Middle Path that includes the central belief that all phenomena are empty of self-existence and dependently co-arisen; "Avalokitesvara"and "Padmasambhava" are two names of popular Bodhisattvas, the former being the Bodhisattva of compassion and the latter being considered the progenitor of Vajrayana Buddhism in Tibet; "Prajnaparamita" means "the Perfection of Wisdom" and also refers to a collection of various Mahayana sutras; "Nirodha-Samapatti" means the attainment of extinction and generally refers to the extinction of feeling and perception through meditation.

231 "The City of the Pyramids" is a name for the Qabalistic Sephirah of Binah which one reaches after successfully crossing the Abyss, i.e. dissolving one's ego in the Absolute. The entire line is also an obscure reference to a certain ceremony. If you want Wisdom, you have to seek it; I can't just give you everything.

232 The "arrow" is a reference to the arrow of Sagittarius, whose Path is attributed to that which reaches up to the Sun of Tiphareth or union with God, as well as to the teaching of the Buddha regarding the poison arrow, i.e. if one is shot with an arrow, one shouldn't ask too many questions about who shot the arrow, its model and make, *et cetera*. One should take practical measures to heal the wound of *dukkha* rather than engaging in fruitless metaphysical speculation.

233 Babalon is the name for the Great Mother who dwells in the City of the Pyramids of Binah, the 3rd Sephirah on the Tree of Life. She is described in the Book of Revelation and Aleister Crowley's *The Vision and the Voice* as having the blood of the saints in the Cup of her fornication 'cause she's kinky like that.

234 "Stream-enterer" is the first of four stages in becoming an Arahant, or liberated one.

235 The "fetters" are mental impediments that keep one bound to *samsara*.

236 Typhon, Hermanubis, and the Sphinx are three Egyptian images that represent the three forms of energy: activity, passivity, and neutrality, which correspond to Rajas, Tamas, and Sattvas in the Hindu system of *gunas* as well as Fire, Water, and Air in the Western system of the classical Elements. The three figures appear on the rim of the Wheel of Fortune in the 10th Tarot Trump called

"Fortune."

237 The "austere vow" is the Bodhisattva vow to renounce one's final release from *samsara* until all beings have achieved enlightenment.

238 The "Double-Wand of Power" in the title is a reference to *Liber AL,* III:72, "I am the Lord of the Double Wand of Power," and in this context refers to the power over duality.

239 The reference to being a priest of Amon-Ra is a gibe at Crowley saying he was a high priest of Mentu named Ankh-af-na-khonsu who created the funerary stele that we now call the Stele of Revealing.

240 The hawk-headed god is, of course, Horus in his specific form as Ra-Hoor-Khuit.

241 "En aat am-a shu-t em neter" comes from the *Egyptian Book of the Dead* and can be translated as "There is no part of me that is not of the gods," which is said in the central ceremony of Ordo Templi Orientis, "Liber XV: The Gnostic Mass."

242 The "Holy Language" here refers to English because *Liber AL vel Legis* is written in English. It is said by Harold sarcastically, in case anyone get angry that the author actually thinks it is holier than any other language.

243 The line regarding the "firmamental fane" is a reference to a speech from Crowley's play "The Ship." It basically means "heavenly temple."

244 "Hale" is a word that means healthy or free from disease, and it has its roots in a world that means "whole." Harold is intentionally mishearing Horus' greeting, a bit of typical Shakespearean comedy.

245 "Budge" refers to E.A. Wallis Budge who was a popular Egyptologist in the early 20th Century and whose work is generally discredited by modern scholars.

246 "Will is a flame...": This is a reference to several lines within *Liber AL vel Legis* where various fiery metaphors are used to describe the Will; it is also a reference to "O secret of secrets that art hidden in the being of all that lives," which is a line from "Liber XV: The Gnostic Mass"; it also is a reference to the fact that, in Western occultism, the Will is often attributed to the Element of Fire and its corresponding magical weapon of the Wand.

247 "Will is pure...": This is a reference to the idea that is exemplified by *Liber AL,* I:44, "Pure will, unassuaged of purpose, delivered from the lust of result, is every way perfect."

248 The "Blasted Tower" refers to the Major Arcana card in the Tarot,

"Atu XVI: The Tower," which depicts a tower being destroyed by lightning or fire and is attributed to the classical Planet of Mars (and Horus is a martial god of War, at least in part).

249 "Will is one-pointed...": This is a reference to Crowley's "nail sermon" in "Liber CL: De Lege Libellum."

250 "Aloof and alone" is a reference to the same phrase used in the Anthem of "Liber XV: The Gnostic Mass."

251 Crushing an universe refers to *Liber AL,* III:72, "...my left hand is empty, for I have crushed an Universe; & nought remains."

252 Chokmah literally means "Wisdom" and is represented by the Phallus as symbolic of the Creative Force. Binah refers to the Great Mother and corresponds with the color black; the black box refers to the Womb or Tabernacle or Throne of God.

253 A reference to *The Book of Lies,* chapter 14.

254 In this metaphor, the blue woman represents Mysticism, blue being the color of aspiration and of Chesed, the Sephirah before the Abyss. The scarlet man represents Magick, the martial force of causing Change in conformity with Will, scarlet or red being the color of descending force and of Geburah, the Sephirah of Mars. The debate is basically an exchange between someone who abides in non-duality/0 (the mystic) and someone who abides in duality/2 (the magician).

255 A quotation from Nietzsche that has an added meaning with a Qabalistic reading thereof.

256 The reference is to the idea that the Mystic travels straight up the Tree of Life on the Middle Pillar without bothering with any of the other Sephiroth. The Magician travels up the Tree of Life Sephirah-by-Sephirah, like a Serpent climbing the Tree slowly.

257 The Wand of the Magician is the Middle Pillar of the Tree of Life. The 3 Paths that connect the Middle Pillar – Gimel, Samkeh, and Tav – forms the word for the Staff of Moses, the rod of almond. Mercy and Severity are the two Pillars on either side of this Middle Pillar.

258 A direct quotation from Oscar Wilde.

259 He was wrong, underestimating the amount of simpletons in the world.

260 A reference to the Gnostic Mass in one sense, but it is also a reference to the comedic play, "The Belly of the Beast."

261 A *Wizard of Oz* joke. How utterly un-serious and un-becoming for

a book on *sutras*!

262 *Liber Librae,* line 0.

263 *Liber AL,* II:71-72.

264 *Liber AL,* II:9.

265 This is based on the *Adittapariyaya Sutta,* more well known as the "Fire Sermon." It was claimed by T.S. Eliot to correspond in importance to the Sermon on the Mount. I personally find that insulting to the Fire Sermon.

266 A reference to how virtually all Buddhist sutras start with the phrase "Thus I have heard." Aside from this showing that this particular writing will be in a "Buddhist mood," the phrase instills a sense of humility insofar as the author is conveying what he has heard rather than asserting it as the inerrant word of God or the Secret Chiefs or whomever else.

267 "Venerable None" is firstly a play on the phrase "Venerable One." This refers to the None/Naught/Nothing/0 of Thelemic philosophy. Also, Qabalistically, Venerable None is V.N., Vav-Nun, which enumerates to 56, the number of Nuit. This number is a combination of 5 & 6, Microcosm and Macrocosm, and therefore a symbol of the Great Work accomplished; Nuit is Herself a symbol of the None.

268 The Master writes in "The Comment Called D" for *Liber AL,* II:9, "The Shadow called Sorrow is caused by the error of thinking of any two Events as opposed or even distinct; which fault was in the first chapter of this Book thus condemned: 'for thereby cometh hurt.'"

269 In the system of O.T.O., these are I° (birth), II° (life), and III° (death).

270 The reference is to *Liber AL,* II:17, "Hear me, ye people of sighing! / The sorrows of pain and regret / Are left to the dead and the dying, / The folk that not know me as yet" and *Liber AL,* II:46, "Dost thou fail? Art thou sorry? Is fear in thine heart?"

271 A reference to the "Fire Sermon" section of T.S. Eliot's *The Wasteland.* You're welcome, Sister.

272 That is, the noble disciple has pierced the Veil of the Abyss and transcended the multiplicity implied by the Sephiroth below the Abyss. Attaining Understanding refers to attaining to the sphere of Binah, which literally means "Understanding." One arises as a Master of the Temple therein, disentangled from all the shadows of the world.

273 This "Nothing" has a double meaning here, emphasized by its capitalization. There is nothing beyond the consciousness of the eye, ear, tongue, nose, body, and mind in the conventional sense – they constitute the entire universe of which we are aware and they are all shadows. All these things constitute our "All," and all of these things "pass & are done." In another sense, there is "Nothing" beyond this All – the undivided, unbounded, infinite Naught or 0 that transcends the multiplicity of All. This is seen in *The Book of the Law* after Hadit curses all things "that perish" and then explains, "This is of the 4: there is a fifth who is invisible, & therein am I as a babe in an egg" (c.f. *AL,* II:49). That is, Hadit likens Himself to Spirit, the Quintessence or fifth Element, that permeates yet transcends the Four Elements. This Spirit is identified with the Nothing, Naught, or 0 insofar as Hadit Himself claims to be identified therewith (c.f. *AL,* II:15, "For I am perfect, being Not").

274 This is based very tangentially on the Diamond Sutra, much more in spirit rather than in letter.

275 Crowley's motto as a Master of the Temple, or Magister Templi 8=3, was V.V.V.V.V., which stands for "Vi Veri Vniversus Vivus Vici" ['By the power of Truth, I have conquered the Universe']. This is also taken as the name as the "Light of the World" itself, which is understood to have manifested through Crowley rather than simply being Crowley the man. Aside from "she" being used here to give a little shock to the reader who inevitably expects a male pronoun, it is said that Aspirants to the A∴A∴ are men and the Brothers of A∴A∴ are women. The setting of the bar shows that V.V.V.V.V. looks and acts like a regular person. Further, the setting of the bar is a reference to the "tavern" that is mentioned in *Liber LXV,* IV:11-14. The bar or tavern refers to the Temple, the bartender is the Hierophant who tends to the draught of Gnosis upon which the patrons become intoxicated. Is not the Oracle on the Bottle "TRINC"?

276 The term "None" is used in the place of "One," for Naught is our ultimate conception, not Unity. Unity or One implies a positive number, a deviation from the infinite None, whereas None or Zero contains all opposites in itself, just as 1 and -1 (or X and -X) combine and annihilate each other in Naught.

277 The call and response shows a harmony or unity between the One of the Master and the Many of the Disciples, reflecting the unity and

identity of None and Two.

278 The point is not to belittle the disciple but to show the question as laughable and absurd.

279 Most Wise Initiatrix is, as an acronym, M.W.I. or Mem-Vav-Yod, which equals 56, the number of Nuit, of whom the Master is a reflection. Qablahblah!

280 *Liber AL*, II:32, "Also reason is a lie; for there is a factor infinite & unknown; & all their words are skew-wise."

281 *Liber LXV*, II:21-22, "Who art thou that dost float and fly and dive and soar in the inane? Behold, these many æons have passed; whence camest thou? Whither wilt thou go? And laughing I chid him, saying: No whence! No whither!"

282 For more on this doctrine concerning knowledge and Under-standing, *ruach* and *neschamah*, see *Little Essays Towards Truth*, especially the essays "Man," "Knowledge," and "Under-standing."

283 The Master has said in *Liber Aleph*, "Keep therefore in just Balance the Relation of Illusion to Illusion in that Aspect of Illusion, neither confusing the Planes, nor confounding the Stars, nor denying the Laws of their Reaction, yet with Eagle's Vision beholding the One Sun of the True Nature of the Whole."

284 For the doctrine concerning Babalon and the draining of blood, see the 12th Aethyr of *The Vision and the Voice*. The Master also explains succinctly in *Liber LXXIII: The Urn*, "In *The Vision and the Voice*, the attainment of the grade of Master of the Temple was symbolized by the adept pouring every drop of his blood, that is his whole individual life, into the Cup of the Scarlet Woman, who represents Universal Impersonal Life."

285 For the doctrine concerning Nemo, see the 13th Aethyr of *The Vision and the Voice*.

286 This phrase comes from the 5th Aethyr of *The Vision and the Voice* and contains an essential doctrine of Understanding.

287 New Comment to *Liber AL*, III:58.

288 "Chief of all" is a phrase that comes from *Liber AL*, I:23, and the quotation from the Master Therion comes from the Old and New Comments thereon.

289 Horus is described as the Crowned and Conquering Child, a designation implied by the name "the noble Master V.V.V.V.V." The fact that these titles apply to things other than Horus is no shock to those whose viewpoint is from above the Abyss; only those below

the Abyss would argue and quarrel over the "correct attribution" thereof.

290 This is a reference to *Liber AL*, II:34, "But ye, o my people, rise up & awake!" The entire doctrine of *Liber AL*, II:27-34, is relevant to this passage.

291 The third penal sign is given by Sabazius X° as, "Place your right hand level, with the thumb extended in a square towards the navel. Draw the hand across the center of the body to the right, drop it to the side, and raise it again to place the point of the thumb upon the navel."

292 The Creed in the Gnostic Mass states, "And I believe in one Earth, the Mother of us all, and in one Womb wherein all men are begotten, and wherein they shall rest, Mystery of Mystery, in Her name BABALON."

293 "Study" does not mean intellectual analysis; it means integrating the words of the text so pervasively into one's being that they become as if they were truths spoken by you.

294 *Liber Cheth vel Vallum Abiegni,* line 21.

295 "Particle of dust" is a reference to *Liber AL*, I:61.

296 This is a reference to the Ceremony of the Opening of the Veil in the Gnostic Mass. This particular part of the Gnostic Mass can be seen as the Crossing of the Abyss to abide in the "deep practice" of the Womb of Babalon, the Perfection of Understanding, with the Lance symbolizing penetrating Wisdom or insight.

297 See *Liber Aleph* for a more detailed explanation of this Word as well as the Words of other Magi.

298 *Liber AL*, I:56.

299 The Eye in the Triangle refers Qabalistically to the Supernal Triangle, the Womb of Babalon, the *sanctum sanctorum,* the Perfection of Understanding.

300 *Liber AL*, II:27.

301 Commentary to *Liber AL*, II:9, in the "Comment Called D."

302 New Comment to *Liber AL*, II:9.

303 Chen-k'o is a Chinese monk of the 16ᵗʰ century who wrote a commentary on the Heart Sutra.

304 The reference is to *Liber AL*, I:22, "Bind nothing! Let there be no difference made among you between any one thing & any other thing; for thereby there cometh hurt."

305 The raised finger of Gu-tei is a reference to the 3ʳᵈ Case in *The*

Gateless Gate, a Zen classic, where it is said, "Whenever Gutei Oshō was asked about Zen, he simply raised his finger. Once a visitor asked Gutei's boy attendant, 'What does your master teach?' The boy too raised his finger. Hearing of this, Gutei cut off the boy's finger with a knife. The boy, screaming with pain, began to run away. Gutei called to him, and when he turned around, Gutei raised his finger. The boy suddenly became enlightened." The flower is a reference to Buddha's so-called "Flower Sermon" that is seen as the beginning of the Zen tradition; one version comes from the 6th Case in *The Gateless Gate* where it is written, "When Shakyamuni Buddha was at Mount Grdhrakuta, he held out a flower to his listeners. Everyone was silent. Only Mahakashyapa broke into a broad smile. The Buddha said, 'I have the True Dharma Eye, the Marvelous Mind of Nirvana, the True Form of the Formless, and the Subtle Dharma Gate, independent of words and transmitted beyond doctrine. This I have entrusted to Mahakashyapa.'"

306 *Liber Tzaddi vel Hamus Hermeticus,* lines 29-30.

307 The Mystic number of 3 is $\Sigma(1\text{-}3) = 1+2+3 = 6$.

308 This comes from the Creed of the Gnostic Mass.

309 *De Lege Libellum sub figura CL.*

310 *De Lege Libellum sub figura CL.*

311 The New Comment to *The Book of the Law* says, "'AL' is the true name of the Book, for these letters, and their number 31, form the Master Key to its Mysteries."

312 *Liber AL,* I:29.

313 Bodhidharma was a Buddhist monk credited with bringing Zen to China who lived from the 5th and 6th centuries C.E.

314 Nagarjuna is the founder of the Madhyamaka school of Buddhism that asserts *shunyata* or emptiness as the fundamental or true nature of things. Ching-chueh was a Zen monk of the 7th and 8th centuries C.E..

315 The first quotation is a reference to *Liber AL,* I:28-30, "None... and two. For I am divided for love's sake, for the chance of union. This is the creation of the world, that the pain of division is as nothing, and the joy of dissolution all." Note that the "pain of division," 2, "is as nothing," 0; and"the joy of dissolution," 0, is "all," 2. 2 is 0 and 0 is 2, All is Naught and Naught is All. What strange Mysteries lie within this mighty and terrible Book!

316 "Solve et coagula" is an alchemical formula and, in this context,

refers to the 2 becoming 0 (*solve*) and the 0 becoming 2 (*coagula*).

317 *The Book of Lies,* chapter 63.

318 *The Book of Lies,* chapter 3.

319 *Liber LXV,* I:53.

320 *Liber V vel Reguli.*

321 *Liber AL,* II:58.

322 *Little Essays Towards Truth,* "Mastery."

323 *Liber AL,* II:6, "I am the flame that burns in every heart of man, and in the core of every star."

324 Fa-tsang was a patriarch of a school of Chinese Buddhism in the 7th and 8th centuries C.E.

325 The reference is to the line of the Creed of the Gnostic Mass that states, "I confess my life one, individual, and eternal, that was, and is, and is to come." This "life" is called the "pure soul" in *Confessions,* chapter 72.

326 Again, the reference is to the line of the Creed of the Gnostic Mass that states, "I confess my life one, individual, and eternal, that was, and is, and is to come."

327 This phrase comes from the opening invocation of the Goetia that was later adapted by Crowley for use in *Liber Samekh.*

328 Consider this in light of the 2nd chapter of the *Tao Te Ching.*

329 *Liber AL,* II:15.

330 Bodhidharma was a Buddhist monk credited with bringing Zen to China who lived from the 5th and 6th centuries C.E.

331 *The Book of Lies,* chapter 5.

332 *Liber AL,* I:22.

333 Hui-ching was a Chinese monk in the 6th and 7th centuries C.E.

334 From Friedrich Nietzsche's *The Gay Science.*

335 *Eight Lectures on Yoga,* "Yoga for Yellowbellies," First Lecture.

336 *The Vision and the Voice,* 1st Aethyr.

337 Hui-ching was a Chinese monk in the 6th and 7th centuries C.E.

338 Bodhidharma was a Buddhist monk credited with bringing Zen to China who lived from the 5th and 6th centuries C.E.

339 *Little Essays Towards Truth,* "Knowledge."

340 Bodhidharma was a Buddhist monk credited with bringing Zen to China who lived from the 5th and 6th centuries C.E.

341 "The Soul of the Desert."

342 *Little Essays Towards Truth,* "Mastery."

343 *Liber AL,* III:17.

344 New Comment to *Liber AL,* III:17.
345 *Liber AL,* I:27.
346 *Liber AL,* I:22, I:52.
347 Old Comment to *Liber AL,* I:52.
348 *Liber AL,* I:45.
349 *Liber AL,* II:46-47.
350 New Comment to *Liber AL,* II:46-47.
351 *Liber AL,* I:22.
352 Djeridensis Comment on *Liber AL,* I:22.
353 *Liber AL,* II:23.
354 *Liber Cheth vel Vallum Abiegni,* line 15.
355 *Magick in Theory and Practice,* chapter 7.
356 *Little Essays Towards Truth,* "Laughter."

CPSIA information can be obtained
at www.ICGtesting.com
Printed in the USA
BVHW080904020123
655389BV00002B/231